Literature Matters

Literature Matters

J. Hillis Miller

Edited by Monika Reif-Hülser

O
OPEN HUMANITIES PRESS

London 2016

First edition published by OPEN HUMANITIES PRESS 2016

Copyright © 2016 J. Hillis Miller and respective rights holders. Please see *Permissions* at the back of this book.

Freely available online at http://openhumanitiespress.org/books/titles/literature-matters

This is an open access book, licensed under Creative Commons By Attribution Share Alike license. Under this license, authors allow anyone to download, reuse, reprint, modify, distribute, and/or copy their work so long as the authors and source are cited and resulting derivative works are licensed under the same or similar license. No permission is required from the authors or the publisher. Statutory fair use and other rights are in no way affected by the above.

Read more about the license at creativecommons.org/licenses/by-sa/4.0

PRINT ISBN 978-1-78542-034-4
PDF ISBN 978-1-78542-035-1

OPEN HUMANITIES PRESS

Open Humanities Press is an international, scholar-led open access publishing collective whose mission is to make leading works of contemporary critical thought freely available worldwide. More at http://openhumanitiespress.org

Contents

Introduction	7
Cold Heaven, Cold Comfort:	15
Should We Read Literature Now, and, If So, How?	31
A Defense Of Literature And Literary Study	54
Ecotechnics	66
Theories of Community	106
Globalization and World Literature	147
Permissions	170

Introduction

My first encounter with J. Hillis Miller dates back to the time when Wolfgang Iser held the chair for English Literature and Literary Theory at the University of Konstanz, Germany, and I was one of Iser's doctoral candidates. Listening to Iser's colleague and friend from Irvine, fascinated by his dedication to reading and to teaching literature, I started to read more of him. Then, one day Wolfgang Iser asked me to prepare, translate, and edit a small book with Hillis Miller's recent lectures on "Illustration" which he had given at Konstanz. *Illustration* was published in German under the title *Illustration. Die Spur der Zeichen in Kunst, Kritik und Kultur* in 1993. This was the beginning of a life-enhancing and enjoyable relationship, which saw the publication of another small book, a lecture by Hillis Miller given on the occasion of Iser's birthday July 21, 2011 with the title *Grenzgänge mit Iser und Coetzee. Literatur lesen—aber wie und wozu?* (2013), and finally led to this collection. All circulate around the question: *why, and what for literature?* Or the same question with a somewhat wider scope: Why and for what the study of culture(s) via the close-reading of texts – if our everyday life world is dominated by electronic media and digital art including the jobs they offer? How is literature received by its readers, what drives the need to constitute its meaning?

This question is not entirely new; there has long been an occasionally competitive relationship between the written word and an image — Miller's book *Illustration* deals extensively with this issue. What makes us look for the hidden order in the chaotic play of the signs? The answers depend on the political, cultural and aesthetic climate of a society. Hence Miller asks in one of his essays, whether we should read literature and if so, how? Not only *that* we should read but also *how* we are supposed to read is the challenge for literary, theoretical, and critical texts alike. Both Wolfgang Iser and Hillis Miller hold the view that *reading literature* opens dimensions of experience which enable us to account for the importance of the 'fictive,' or the 'fictional' in individual and social life. One of the most important experiences literature provides, according to Iser, is to bring into focus the eccentric position of the human being, "who is, but does not have himself."[1] The same is true for what is called "meaning," which is itself subjected to change by constantly mutating demands of acculturation. 'Acts of fictionalization'— to use one of Iser's terms—have the creative and formative power to link the *Real* and the *Imaginary* in such a way that experiences coined through reading can be amalgamated with experiences from the life world and hence open up new, retrospective views on it. Or, to put it in Hillis Miller's words: "We read because literary texts provide us with imaginative worlds which enable us to fuse together various facets of the Real." It is a particular kind of gain we receive through this fusion: the Real turns into the Known and the Unknown at the same moment.

Literature Matters Today

Just as I was finalizing my translations and the structure of this book, a new text reached me entitled "Literature Matters Today."[2] The title is instructive. It is undoubtedly an intentionally plurivalent expression which evokes many thematic conjunctions, branching, references—without directly naming them. That article formed the beginning of the guiding "red thread," which runs through the entire collection despite its manifold topics and observations, its critical stances, and wide interests. J. Hillis Miller used the metaphor of "the red thread" already in 1992, with the appearance of his book *Ariadne's Thread: Story Lines*.[3]

"Literature Matters Today"—a question raises itself at once: which word is the verb? Is there a verb at all? Why would it matter? If "Matters" is read as a verb, the sentence is an assertion and seems to answer Miller's following reflections "Why Literature?" If "Matters" is read as a noun, we understand it in the sense of business, concern, or case of literature. In any case, the expression focuses on the idea that literature produces effects; it will thus change and influence the thoughts of those who concern themselves with it and, hence, it will also change the world.

In order to deal with the issue of effects or consequences of literature on life, Hillis Miller resorts to his own intellectual biography; he calls it a "commitment" which brings him very close to his readers. He argues that the unique feature of literature, developed over the course of European cultural history from the seventeenth century on, increasingly diminishes in the 21st century because its message is taken over by other media. At this point of the argument, we remember the puzzling title "Literature Matters Today" and assume that the power of the "Matters of Literature today" lies precisely in recognizing and critically evaluating *that* and *how* we experience the workings of different media on our mind.

The first chapter raises the question explicitly in its title: "Should we read and teach literature today?" In particular, it addresses high school and university decisions such as privileging particular departments by granting financial means, personnel decisions, job guaranties, career oriented shifting of task definitions, etc. Being able to "read" literary texts, Hillis Miller indicates, implies the skill of decoding messages behind the façade of rhetoric, so that the 'what is meant' can be discovered in the 'strategies of meaning'.

The second chapter focuses on the issue of border crossing in Wolfgang Iser's theory of fiction and anthropology in relation to J.M. Coetzee's novel *Waiting for the Barbarians*. This novel is a story about the dialectics of power and impotence, about the tensions and possible insights into knowledge arising out of the forceful encounter of the two antagonistic principles. Step by step, Hillis Miller displays in what ways *close reading* unfolds in the encounter of text and reader. In particular Miller shows convincingly that there is no difference in the procedure of constituting meaning if we read a literary, aesthetically constructed text like Coetzee's *Waiting for the Barbarians* or if we approach and try to 'decode' the message of a theoretical text such as Iser's *The Fictive and the Imaginary*. It is the process of associating meaning with theoretical configurations that attracts Hillis Miller's attention: "how should we learn to read if we are not trained anymore to decode the multidimensionality and complexity of rhetorical figures?"

Chapter three deals with the semantic field of "Globalization" as a concept; it tries to define the corner points within which literary studies moves in light of Globalization. Closely linked with this in Miller's argument are tele-technologies and the particular forms of the 'Real' they produce. Jacques Derrida's made-up-word for this artificial 'Real' is *artefactualities*. Just as "matter" plays with the new combinatory possibilities of "art" and "world," so too does Derrida's coinage, which in fact harks back to Wittgenstein's well-known statement: "the world is everything that is the case." It must have been television that was on Derrida's mind when he thought of *artefactuality*, says Hillis Miller. "The images provided not only by the new media but also by the old ones, appear to be facts, yet they are products." Hillis Miller unwraps the "totally other" of literature as soon as he opens his exemplary reading of Wallace Stevens's poem "The River of Rivers in Connecticut." Although the 'real' banks of the river as described in the poem do exist, although the literary representation provokes effects of recognition, there is, nevertheless, the constant de-familiarization of the familiar, the disturbing realization of the incessantly changing well-known. "We cannot see the river of rivers in Connecticut outside or beyond the language which narrates it."

In chapter four, the influences of technology on the humanities are what is at stake. Here Hillis Miller engages in an intensive discussion of the term "Eco-Technology," and the idea of considering technology as a model for the Humanities once we start reflecting on the actual state of affairs in the world. Here the focus is on the world as our living environment which we change according to our actual needs without knowing how to stop the transformations should they prove dangerous to us, to others, to the globe. To illustrate his argument, Miller chooses a very brief yet all the more intricate story by Franz Kafka in order to demonstrate via *close reading* what—and, if so, how—the shift from an organic to a technological model of interpretation would look like. Miller reads Kafka's story, or perhaps better "text-reflection," titled *Die Sorge des Hausvaters* (from 1919, 474 words), as a playing field to test the consequences of such a shift from an organic unity to a technological model.

With this question we entered the realm of "destructuralizing structures," auto-generating systems, equivalent to those which Hillis Miller sees in the "Earth," the "global finance system," a "community" or a "nation," in the "Eco-system" and the "body system" from which the term "auto-immunity" is borrowed.

"The Conflagration of Community" (chapter 5)[4] turns directly to the issue of writing, literature, and to their legitimation in difficult times. Miller's reflections for this long chapter start with a critical reading of the well-known statement by Theodor Adorno, "writing a poem after

Auschwitz is barbaric."⁵ For Miller, this is the point where he decisively addresses the issue of ethics in the Humanities. His paradigmatic texts are those which present and represent topics of community and society, the effects of the Holocaust on these congregations, the living together of individual humans under the declared commitment of respect and recognition, even if there are different attitudes towards common interests. It is historical witnessing and the literary vision of such witnessing that interests Miller. What follows is an engaged and engaging reading of novelistic representations of the Holocaust which are compared with fictional texts written before and after Auschwitz. He is interested in the similarities and echoes of these texts with recently published theoretical considerations of the effects of the Holocaust on the condition of terms of community and society. Kafka foreshadows Auschwitz, Kertézs' *Fatelessness* echoes Kafka and Toni Morrison's novel *Beloved* is also a post-Auschwitz novel with Kafkaesque traits.

No reading is completely disinterested or objective; reading is always geared to answer significant and destined questions. Hence if one of the important questions enquires into the meaning of "conflagration of community" in the twentieth century—the next question must address what it means to call the novels under discussion acts of witnessing. Here Miller constantly comes back to the function and effectiveness of speech acts for and in conflagrant societies. Finally, he is haunted by the question of the possible resonances between the difficulties of imaging, understanding, indeed remembering Auschwitz at all—a frequent theme in historical and fictional records—and the earlier-discussed novels' unnerving reservation towards clear-cut, coherent interpretations as manifested by Kafka, Kertész and Morrison. All of these texts evoke personal dismay and sadness and are, hence, not simply intellectually distanced, academic subjects. The consternation is caused, as Miller convincingly argues, by contemporary US-American history: Abu Graib, Guantánamo Bay, the unusual surrendering of American captives to the prisons of the American Secret Services throughout the world, the illegal observation of US citizens, etc. Even under Barack Obama's presidency these practices did not really change. More than ever before the dictum seems to prove true, that those who forget history are doomed to repeat it. In this sense the fictional texts discussed here are one way of studying history.

The last chapter, *Globalization and World-Literature*, faces this uneasiness with respect to what Nietzsche calls "Weltliteratur"—a term Miller changes in scope by inserting a little hyphen between Welt- and Literature and thus revaluates Nietzsche's expression by turning it into a critical category. But what can Welt-Literatur, in English *World-Literature*, mean? In what language should it be written? What are its key aspects? Isn't there some kind of all-embracing similarity among the inhabitants of the *Global Village* as far as life-style and mode of work is concerned? Are the members of the academic jet-set "translated men," as Edward Said and Salman Rushdie called themselves? Where is the borderline of cultural imperialism?

If we take the term World-Literature in Miller's sense, with a hyphen and the stress on both parts—"world" and "literature"—it is not a matter of course in every part of the world. As in all the essays collected here, Miller develops his literary critical observations *as* cultural criticism formulated along the individual reading processes of each concrete example. Thus in this last chapter we recall Miller's literary critical considerations in his close reading of W.B. Yeats' poem "The Cold Heaven." In his interpretation of Yeats' poem, Miller focused on the politically willed situation of American high school management. Here he asks what happens if a poem, a text, a genre-oriented construction of language and meaning is transposed into another linguistic and semantic system. Does it stay the same, how semantically significant are the changes? The transposition of a sentence, a phrase, a word into another language depends on the realm of imaginative figurations which the other culture offers for the implementation of an imaginative coherency. For an adequate translation, Miller enlists fifteen criteria or points to be taken into consideration, which is already a remarkable number.

Miller's ideas found support at a recent conference in Shanghai centred on Nietzsche's essay "On the advantage and disadvantage of history for life." As Miller reports, it was interesting for him to hear different interpretations both "for and against" the applicability of this phrase when considering the difference of experience in Western and Eastern thought. What did Nietzsche mean with "Weltliteratur"? The answer to that question was not to be found.

In the debate over the similarities and significant differences between *Weltliteratur* in Nietzsche's understanding, and *World-Literature* in Milller's sense, there were many captivating ideas about the adaptability of theorems such as *Intertextuality, Interculturality, Internationalization*—in short: the simple question of *translatability* of ideas from one cultural context into another. What does *Inter-* mean, and how does *Trans-* work in communicative processes? When, for instance, Nietzsche expresses his enthusiasm for Ralph Waldo Emerson's formulations about the importance of history and we read this dialogue today, then the communication among partners takes place through time and space. It is in particular Emerson's essay *Nature* (1836) in which Nietzsche found his own ideas about the importance of history for life, published in 1874 *pre*-formulated.

Emerson's text starts with the following sentences:

> Our age is retrospective. It builds the sepulchres of the fathers. It writes biographies, histories, and criticism. The foregoing generations beheld God and nature face to face; we, through their eyes. Why should not we also enjoy an original relation to the universe? Why should not we have a poetry and philosophy of insight and not of tradition, and a religion by revelation to us, and not the history of theirs? … why should we grope among the dry bones of the past, or put the living generation into masquerade out of its faded wardrobe? The sun shines to-day also. There is more wool and flax in the fields. There are new lands, new men, new thoughts. Let us demand our own works and laws and worship.

※

J. Hillis Miller is an academic, a teacher, a classicist of literature, a critic who knows how to read the signs of the times. And his analytical thinking is not somewhere in the clouds but closely attached to the burning questions of our times such as climate change, migration, economics and knowledge management, to name just a few that appear in this collection of essays. He understands his encounters with literature, no matter how great the historical distance, as interventions to the present. As such he offers them to his readers.

September, 2015
Monika Reif-Hülser

Notes

1. Wolfgang Iser, *Das Fiktive und das Imaginäre. Perspektiven literarischer Anthropologie* (Frankfurt am Main: Suhrkamp, 1991), 505.

2. In *SubStance* # 131, Vol. 42, no. 12, (2013).

3. J. Hillis Miller, *Ariadne's Thread: Story Lines* (New Haven: Yale University Press, 1992).

4. See Miller, *The Conflagration of Community: Fiction before and after Auschwitz* (Chicago: University of Chicago Press, 2011).

5. Theodor W. Adorno, "Kulturkritik und Gesellschaft," *Prismen : Kulturkritik und Gesellschaft* (Munich: dtv, 1963), 7-26.

I

Cold Heaven, Cold Comfort: Should We Read or Teach Literature Now?

> ... *an entire epoch of so-called literature, if not all of it, cannot survive a certain technological regime of telecommunications (in this respect the political regime is secondary). Neither can philosophy, or psychoanalysis. Or love letters.*
>
> Jacques Derrida, "Envois," in *The Post Card*

By "we" in my title I mean we students, teachers, and the ordinary citizens of our "global village," if such a term still means anything. By "read" I mean careful attention to the text at hand, that is, "close reading." By "literature" I mean printed novels, poems, and plays. By "now" I mean the hot summer of 2010, when I first drafted this essay. That summer was the culmination of the hottest six months on record, clear evidence for those who have bodies to feel of global warming. Now in 2013 the evidence for global warming is even less refutable, with more and more violent storms, droughts, tornadoes, floods, melting ice sheets, and so on. Even the cold winter of 2012-13 is said by scientists to be caused by the destruction, brought about by melting arctic ice, of the atmospheric shield that used to protect us from Arctic cold. I mean also the time of slowly receding global financial crisis and worldwide deep recession. I mean the time of desktop computers, the Internet, iPhones, iPads, DVDs, MP3s, Facebook, Twitter, Google, computer games by the thousand, television, and a global film industry. I mean the time when colleges and universities are, in the United States at least, losing funding and are shifting more and more to a corporate model. As one result of these changes, at least 70% of university teaching in the United States in all fields is now done by adjuncts, that is, by people who not only do not have tenure but who also have no possibility of getting it. They are not "tenure track." By "now" I mean a time when calls on all sides, from President Obama on down in the government and by the media left and right, are being made for more and better teaching of math, science, and engineering, while hardly anyone calls for more and better teaching in the humanities. The humanities, as a high administrator at Harvard, perhaps its then president, Lawrence Summers, is reported to have said, "are a lost cause."

Should or ought we to read or teach literature in such a "now"? Is it an ethical obligation to do so? If so, which works? How should these be read, and who should teach them?

During the nineteen years I taught at the Johns Hopkins University, from 1953 to 1972, I would have had ready answers to these questions. These answers would have represented our unquestioned consensus at Hopkins about the nature and mission of the humanities. A (somewhat absurd) ideological defense of literary study, especially study of British literature, was pretty firmly in place at Hopkins during those years. We in the English Department had easy consciences because we thought we were doing two things that were good for the country: a) teaching young citizens the basic American ethos (primarily by way of the literature of a foreign country [England] we defeated in a revolutionary war of independence; the absurdity of that project only recently got through to me); b) doing research that was like that of our scientific colleagues in that it was finding out the "truth" about the fields covered by our disciplines: languages, literatures, art, history, philosophy. *Veritas vos liberabit*, the truth shall make you free, is the motto of Hopkins (a quotation from the Bible, by the way, something said by Jesus [John 8: 32], in which "truth" hardly means scientific truth). *Lux et veritas*, light and truth, is the motto of Yale. Just plain *Veritas* is Harvard's slogan. Truth, we at Hopkins believed, having forgotten the source of our motto, included objective truth of every sort, for example the truth about the early poetry of Alfred Tennyson or about the poetry of Barnaby Googe. Such truth was a good in itself, like knowledge of black holes or of genetics.

Hopkins, as is well-known, was the first facility to be designated exclusively a "research university" in the United States. It was founded on the model of the great German research universities of the nineteenth century. In literary study that meant inheritance of the German tradition of Romance Philology, Germanic Philology (which included English literature), and Classical Philology, all of which flourished at Hopkins. Such research needed no further justification beyond the intrinsic value accorded to the search for truth and the not entirely persuasive assumption that humanities scholars who were doing that kind of research would be better teachers of literature as the precious repository of our national values. The word "research" was our collective leitmotif. Every professor at Hopkins was supposed to spend 50% of his (we were almost all men) time doing research in his field of specialty. That included humanities professors.

Hopkins was to an amazing degree run by the professors, or at least it seemed so to us. Professors made decisions about hiring, promotion, and the establishment of new programs through a group called the "Academic Council." They were elected by the faculty. Though there was no established quota, the Council always included humanists and social scientists as well as scientists. That means the scientists, who could have outvoted the humanists, were cheerfully electing humanists. Outside support for research at Hopkins came not from industry, but primarily from government agencies like the National Science Foundation, the National Institutes of Health, the National Defense Education Act, and the National Endowment for the Humanities. We benefitted greatly from the Cold War mentality that thought the United States should be best in everything, including even the humanities. None of the teaching was done by adjuncts, though graduate students taught composition and discussion sections of large lecture courses. Most students who received the PhD obtained good tenure track appointments. Misleading statistics even indicated that a shortage of PhD's in the humanities was about to happen, so the English Department at Hopkins briefly instituted a three-year PhD in that field. Two of my own students finished such a PhD and went on to hold professorships at important universities. That shows a PhD in English need not take twelve years or more, the average time today.

Hopkins was in my time there a kind of paradise for professors who happened to be interested in research as well as in teaching. Hopkins then was the closest thing I know to Jacques Derrida's nobly idealistic vision in 2001 of a "university without condition," a university centered on the humanities and devoted to a disinterested search for truth in all areas.[1] It is a great irony that Derrida's little book was delivered as a President's Lecture at Stanford University, since Stanford is one of the great United States elite private universities that is and always has been deeply intertwined with corporate America and, by way of the Hoover Institution, located at Stanford, with the most conservative side of American politics.

Well, what was wrong with Hopkins in those halcyon days? Quite a lot. Practically no women were on the faculty, not even in non-tenured positions"—not a single one in the English Department during all my nineteen years at Hopkins. The education of graduate students in English was brutally competitive, with a high rate of attrition, often by way of withdrawal by the faculty of fellowship funds initially granted to students who were later judged not to be performing well. Some students we "encouraged to leave" took PhDs elsewhere and had brilliant careers as professors of English. Hopkins, finally, was up to its ears in military research at the Applied Physics Laboratory. The Johns Hopkins School of Advanced International Studies was not then, and still is not today, what one would call a model of liberal thinking. Even so, Hopkins was a wonderful place to be a professor of the humanities in the 'fifties and 'sixties.

※

Now, over fifty years later, everything is different in U.S. universities and colleges from what it was at Hopkins when I taught there, as almost everyone involved knows quite well. Even in the 'fifties and 'sixties Hopkins was the exception, not the rule. Nowadays, over 70% of the teaching, as I have said, is done by adjuncts without prospects of tenure. Often they are deliberately kept at appointments just below half-time, so they do not have medical benefits, pension contributions, or other benefits. All three of my children hold doctorates, as does one grandchild, and none of the four has ever held a tenure track position, much less achieved tenure. Tenure track positions in the humanities are few and far between, with hundreds of applicants for each one, and an ever-accumulating reservoir of unemployed humanities PhDs. Funding for the humanities has shrunk both at public and private colleges and universities, as has financial support for universities and colleges generally. Books by Marc Bousquet,

Christopher Newfield, and Frank Donoghue, among others, have told in detail the story of the way U.S. universities have come to be run more and more like corporations governed by the financial bottom line, or, as Peggy Kamuf puts it, the "bang for the buck."[2] The humanities cannot be shown to produce much bang at all. Universities have consequently become more and more trade schools offering vocational training for positions in business, engineering, biology, law, medicine, or computer science. The weakening of American public universities has been accompanied by a spectacular rise in for-profit and partly online universities like the University of Phoenix. These are openly committed to training that will get you a job. John Sperling, the head of the Apollo Group that developed the University of Phoenix, says that Phoenix "is a corporation. . . . Coming here is not a rite of passage. We are not trying to develop [students'] value systems or go in for that 'expand their minds' bullshit."[3] The President of Yale University, Richard Levin, an economist, in a lecture given several years ago before the Royal Society in London, "The Rise of Asia's Universities,"[4] enthusiastically praises China for more than doubling its institutions of higher education (from 1,022 to 2,263), for increasing the number of higher education students from 1 million in 1997 to more than 5.5 million in 2007, and for setting out deliberately to create a number of world-class research universities that will rank with Harvard, M.I.T., Oxford, and Cambridge. The numbers Levin cites are no doubt far higher now. Levin's emphasis, however, is all on the way China's increased teaching of math, science, and engineering will make it more highly competitive in the global economy than it already is. Levin, in spite of Yale's notorious strength in the humanities, says nothing whatsoever about humanities teaching or its utility either in China or in the United States. Clearly the humanities are of no account in the story he is telling. It is extremely difficult to demonstrate that humanities departments bring any financial return at all or that majoring in English is preparation for anything but a low-level service job or a low-paying job teaching English. Many students at elite places like Yale could safely major in the humanities because they would take over their father's business when they graduated, or would go on to law school or business school and get their vocational training there. Lifelong friendships with others who would come to be important in business, government, or the military were in any case more important than any vocational training. The presidential race between George W. Bush and John Kerry was, somewhat absurdly, between two men who did not do all that well academically at Yale but who were members of Yale's most elite secret society, Skull and Bones. Whoever won, Yale and the political power of the Skull and Bones network would win.

Enrollments in humanities courses and numbers of majors have, not surprisingly, especially at less elite places, shrunk to a tiny percentage of the undergraduate and graduate population.[5] Only composition and beginning language courses plus required distribution courses are doing well in the humanities. Legislators, boards of trustees, and university administrators have taken advantage of the recent catastrophic recession to take more control over universities, to downsize and to manage what is taught. The state of California, for example, was, until recently, broke. That meant frozen positions, reduced adjunct funding, and salary reductions for faculty and staff in the great University of California system of between five and ten percent, depending on rank. Teaching loads were increased for above scale professors, that is, for the ones who have done the most distinguished research and who have been rewarded by being given more time to do that. The humanities especially suffered.

❦

This is the not-entirely cheerful situation in which my questions, "Should we read or teach literature now? Do we have an ethical obligation to do so?" must be asked and an attempt to answer them made. How did this disappearance of the justification for literary study happen? I suggest three reasons:

1. The conviction that everybody ought to read literature because it embodies the ethos of our citizens has almost completely vanished. Few people any longer really believe, in their heart of hearts, that it is necessary to read *Beowulf*, Shakespeare, Milton, Samuel Johnson, Wordsworth, Dickens, Woolf and Conrad in order to become a good citizen of the United States.

2. A massive shift in dominant media away from printed books to all forms of digital media, what I call "prestidigitalization," has meant

that literature in the old-fashioned sense of printed novels, poems, and dramas plays a smaller and smaller role in determining the ethos of our citizens. Middle class readers in Victorian England learned how to behave in courtship and marriage by entering into the fictive worlds of novels by Charles Dickens, George Eliot, Anthony Trollope, Elizabeth Gaskell, and many others. Now people satisfy their needs for imaginary or virtual realities by watching films, television, DVDs, playing computer games, and listening to popular music. It was announced on July 19, 2010 by Amazon that for the first time they are selling more e-books to be read on iPads or the Kindle than hardcover printed books. A high point of the summer of 2010 for a colleague and friend of mine in Norway, a distinguished humanities professor, was his trip to Rotterdam to hear a Stevie Wonder concert at the North Sea Jazz Festival, followed by repeat performance of the same concert in his home town of Bergen. He emailed me with great excitement and enthusiasm about these concerts. Stevie Wonder is obviously of great importance in shaping this humanist's "ethos." Whenever I give a lecture on some literary work in any place in the world, members of my audience, especially the younger ones, always want to ask me questions about the film of that work, if a film has been made.

3. The rise of new media has meant more and more the substitution of cultural studies for old-fashioned literary studies. It is natural for young people to want to teach and write about things that interest them, for example, film, popular culture, women's studies, African-American studies, and so on. Many, if not most, U.S. departments of English these days are actually departments of cultural studies, whatever they may go on calling themselves. Little literature is taught these days in American departments of English. Soon Chinese students of English literature, American literature, and worldwide literature in English will know more about these than our indigenous students do. A list several years ago of new books published at the University of Minnesota Press in "Literature and Cultural Studies" did not have one single book on literature proper.

Just to give three examples out of hundreds of career-orientation shifts: Edward Said began as a specialist on the novels and short stories of Joseph Conrad. He went on to write a book that is theory-oriented, *Beginnings,* but his great fame and influence rests on political books like *Orientalism, The Question of Palestine,* and *Culture and Imperialism.* Second, quite different, example: Joan DeJean is a distinguished Professor of Romance Languages at the University of Pennsylvania, but she does not write about French literature in the old-fashioned sense of plays by Racine, novels by Marivaux or Flaubert, poems by Baudelaire, or novels by Duras (all men but Duras, please note). Her influential books include, among others, *The Essence of Style: How the French Invented High Fashion, Fine Food, Chic Cafes, Style, Sophistication* and *The Age of Comfort: When Paris Discovered Casual – and the Modern Home Began.* In short, Professor DeJean does cultural studies, with a feminist slant. Third example: Frank Donoghue began his career as a specialist in 18th-century English literature. He published in 1996 a fine book on *The Fame Machine: Book Reviewing and Eighteenth-Century Literary Careers.* Around 2000 Donoghue shifted to an interest in the current state of the humanities in American universities. In 2008 he published *The Last Professors: The Corporate University and the Fate of the Humanities.* Now he lectures frequently all over the United States as an expert on the corporatizing of the American university.

⚜

I have briefly sketched the present-day situation in the United States within which the question "Should We Read or Teach Literature Now?" must be asked: smaller and smaller actual influence of literature on common culture; fewer and fewer professors who teach literature as opposed to cultural studies; fewer and fewer tenured professors of literature in any case; fewer and fewer books of literary criticism published, and tiny sales for those that are published; radically reduced enrollment in literature courses in our colleges and universities; rapid reduction of literature departments to service departments teaching composition and the rudiments of foreign languages and foreign cultures.

The usual response by embattled humanists is to wring their hands, become defensive, and say literature ought to be taught because we need to know our cultural past, or need to "expand our minds," or need the ethical teaching we can get from literary works. Presidents of the Modern Language Association of America have in their presidential addresses over the decades echoed what Matthew Arnold said about the need to know, as he puts it in *Culture and Anarchy* (1869) "the best that has been thought and said in the world." Robert Scholes, for example, in his 2004 MLA Presidential address, asserted: "We need to show that our learning is worth something by . . . broadening the minds of our students and helping our fellow citizens to more thoughtful interpretations of the crucial texts that shape our culture. . . . We have nothing to offer but the sweetness of reason and the light of learning."[6] "Sweetness and light" is of course Arnold's repeated phrase, in *Culture and Anarchy,* for what culture gives. That book was required reading in the Freshman English course all students took at Oberlin College when I became a student there in 1944.

I think the noble Arnoldian view of the benefits of literary study is pretty well dead and gone these days. For one thing, we now recognize more clearly how problematic and heterogeneous the literary tradition of the West actually is. It by no means teaches some unified ethos, and many of its greatest works are hardly uplifting, including, for example, Shakespeare's *King Lear*. About reading *King Lear*, the poet John Keats, said in a sonnet, "On Sitting Down to Read King Lear Once Again": "For once again the fierce dispute,/Betwixt damnation and impassion'd clay/ Must I burn through."[7] As for Keats himself, Matthew Arnold wrote to his friend Clough, "What a brute you were to tell me to read Keats' letters. However, it is over now: and reflexion resumes her power over agitation."[8] Neither work seemed to their readers all that edifying. Nor is American literature much better. Of one of our great classics, *Moby Dick*, its author, Herman Melville, said, "I have written a wicked book." Furthermore, it is not at all clear to me how reading Shakespeare, Keats, Dickens, Whitman, Yeats, or Wallace Stevens is any use in helping our students to deal with the urgent problems that confront us all these days in the United States: climate change that may soon make the species *homo sapiens* extinct; a deep global recession and catastrophic unemployment (20 million still out of work or underemployed) brought on by the folly and greed of our politicians and financiers; news media like *Fox News* that are more or less lying propaganda arms of our right wing party but are believed in as truth by many innocent citizens; a seemingly endless and unwinnable war in Afghanistan—we all know these problems. Young people in the United States need to get training that will help them get a job and avoid starving to death. They might benefit from courses that would teach them how to tell truth from falsehood on Internet postings.[9] Well, why should we read and teach literature now, in these dire circumstances? I shall return to this question.

※

In order to make this question less abstract, I shall confront my question by way of a short poem by W. B. Yeats. I greatly admire this poem. It moves me greatly. It moves me so much that I want not only to read it but also to teach it and talk about it to anyone who will listen. The poem is called "The Cold Heaven." It is from Yeats's volume of poems of 1916, "Responsibilities." Here is the poem:

The Cold Heaven

> Suddenly I saw the cold and rook-delighting heaven
> That seemed as though ice burned and was but the more ice,
> And thereupon imagination and heart were driven
> So wild that every casual thought of that and this
> Vanished, and left but memories, that should be out of season
> With the hot blood of youth, of love crossed long ago;
> And I took all the blame out of all sense and reason,
> Until I cried and trembled and rocked to and fro,
> Riddled with light. Ah! when the ghost begins to quicken,
> Confusion of the death-bed over, is it sent
> Out naked on the roads, as the books say, and stricken
> By the injustice of the skies for punishment?[10]

I long ago wrote a full essay on this poem.[11] I have discussed it briefly again more recently at a conference on World Literature at Shanghai Jiao Tong University. At Jiao Tong I used Yeats's poem as an example of how difficult it is to transfer a poem from one culture to a different one.

Now I want to consider the poem as a paradigmatic exemplification of the difficulties of deciding whether we should read or teach literature now. Should I read or teach this poem now? My answer is that there is no "should" about it, no compelling obligation or responsibility. I can read or teach it if I like, but that decision cannot be justified by anything beyond the call the poem itself makes on me to read it and teach it. Least of all do I think I can tell students or administrators with a straight face that reading the poem or hearing me teach it is going to help them find a job, or help them mitigate climate change, or help them resist the lies told by the media, though I suppose being a good reader might conceivably aid resistance to lies. Reading the poem or teaching it is, however, a good in itself, an end in itself, as Kant said all art is. The mystical poet Angelus Silesius (1624-77) affirmed, in *The Cherubic Wanderer,* that "The rose is without why." Like that rose, "The Cold Heaven" is without why. The poem, like a rose, has no reason for being beyond itself. You can read it or not read it, as you like. It is its own end. Young people these days who watch films or play computer games or listen to popular music do not, for the most part, attempt to justify what they do. They do it because they like to do it and because it gives them pleasure. My academic friend from Bergen did not try to justify his great pleasure and excitement in hearing at great expense the same Stevie Wonder concert twice, once in Rotterdam and once again in Bergen. He just emailed me his great enthusiasm about the experience. It was a big deal for him, just as reading, talking, or writing about Yeats's "The Cold Heaven" is a big deal for me. That importance, however, is something I should not try to justify by its practical utility. If I do make that attempt I am bound to fail.

A natural response when I see a film I like or hear a concert that moves me is to want to tell other people about it, as my correspondent in Bergen wanted to tell everybody about those Stevie Wonder concerts. These tellings most often take the form, "Wow! I saw a wonderful movie last night. Let me tell you about it." I suggest that my desire to teach Yeats's "The Cold Heaven" takes much the same form: "Wow! I have just read a wonderful poem by Yeats. Let me read it to you and tell you about it." That telling, naturally enough, takes the form of wanting to pass on what I think other readers might find helpful to lead them to respond to the poem as enthusiastically as I do.

I list, in an order following that of the poem, some of the things that might need to be explained not only to a Chinese reader, but also, no doubt, to a computer-games-playing Western young person ignorant of European poetry. David Damrosch recognizes with equanimity, as do I, that when a given piece of literature circulates into a different culture from that of its origin, it will be read differently. I am not talking here, however, about a high-level culturally embedded reading, but just about making sense of Yeats's poem. This need to make sense might arise, for example, in trying to decide how to translate this or that phrase into Chinese. Here are some things it might be good to know when trying to understand "The Cold Heaven": 1) Something about Yeats's life and works; 2) An explanation of the verse form used: three iambic hexameter quatrains rhyming abab. Is it an odd sort of sonnet in hexameters rather than pentameters, and missing the last couplet?; 3) Knowledge of the recurrent use of "sudden" or "suddenly" in Yeats's lyrics; 4) What sort of bird a rook is and why they are delighted by cold weather; 5) The double meaning of "heaven," as "skies" and as the supernatural realm beyond the skies, as in the opening of the Lord's Prayer, said daily by millions of Christians: "Our Father who art in heaven"; compare "skies" at the end: "the injustice of the skies for punishment"; 6) An explanation of oxymorons (burning ice) and of the history in Western poetry of this particular one; 7) Attempt to explain the semantic difference between "imagination" and "heart," as well as the nuances of each word; 8) Explanation of "crossed" in "memories . . . of love crossed long ago," both the allusion to Shakespeare's Romeo and Juliet as "star-crossed lovers," that is, as fated by the stars to disaster in love, and the reference to the biographical fact of Yeats's disastrous love for Maud Gonne: she turned him down repeatedly, so it is to some degree absurd for him to take responsibility for the failure of their love; he did his best to woo her; 9) Account of the difference between "sense" and "reason" in "I took the blame out of all sense and reason," or is this just tautological? A. Norman Jeffares cites T. R. Henn's explanation that "'out of all sense' is an Irish (and ambiguous) expression meaning both 'to an extent far beyond what common sense could justify' and 'beyond the reach of sensation'"[12]; 10) Explanation of the double meaning of the verb "riddle" in the marvelous phrase, "riddled with light": "riddle" as punctured with holes and "riddle" as having a perhaps unanswered riddle or conundrum posed to one; being riddled with light is paradoxical because light is supposed to be illuminating, not obscuring; 11) Unsnarling of the lines centering on "quicken" in "when the ghost [meaning disembodied soul] begins to quicken,/Confusion of the death bed over"; "quicken" usually refers to the coming to life of the fertilized egg in the womb, so an erotic love-bed scene is superimposed on the death-bed one; 12) "as the books say": which books?; all those esoteric books and folklore booksYeats delighted in reading; 13) Relate "injustice of the skies for punishment" to the usual assumption that heaven only punishes justly, gives us our just desserts after death; why and how can the skies be unjust? By blaming him for something that was not his fault? Relate this to Greek and later tragedy. It is not Oedipus's fault that he has killed his father and fathered children on his mother, or is it?; 14) Why is the last sentence a question? Is it a real question or a merely rhetorical one? Would the answer find its place if the blank that follows the twelve lines of this defective sonnet were filled? The poem seems both too much in line lengths and too little in number of lines; 15) Finally, readers might like to know, or might even observe on their own, that Yeats, like other European poets of his generation, was influenced in this poem and elsewhere by what he knew, through translations, of Chinese poetry and Chinese ways of thinking. The volume *Responsibilities*, which contains "The Cold Heaven," has an epigraph from someone Yeats calls, somewhat pretentiously, "Khoung-Fou-Tseu," presumably Confucius: "How am I fallen from myself, for a long time now/I have not seen the Prince of Chang in my dreams" (*Variorum Poems*, 269). Chinese readers might have a lot to say about this Chinese connection and about how it makes "The Cold Heaven" a work of world literature.

All this information would be given to my hearers or readers, however, not to "expand their minds," but in the hope that it might help them admire the poem as much as I do and be moved by it as much as I am. Yeats's poem can hardly be described as "uplifting," since its thematic climax is a claim that the skies are unjust and punish people for things of which they are not guilty. That is a terrifying wisdom. Telling others about this poem is not something I *should* do but something I cannot help doing, something the poem urgently calls on me to do.

Do I think much future exists in U.S. colleges and universities or in our journals and university presses for such readings? No, I do not. I think this dimming of the future for literary studies has been brought about partly by the turning of our colleges and universities into trade schools, preparation for getting a job, institutions that have less and less place for the humanities, but perhaps even more by the amazingly rapid development of new teletechnologies that are fast making literature obsolete, a thing of the past. Even many of those who could teach literature, who were hired to do so, choose rather to teach cultural studies instead: fashion design, or the history of Western imperialism, or film, or some one or another among those myriad other interests that have replaced literature.

I add in conclusion, however, somewhat timidly and tentatively, one possible use studying literature and literary theory might have, or ought to have, in these bad days. Citizens, in the United States at least, are these days inundated with a torrent of distortions and outright lies from politicians, the news media, and advertising on television and radio. Even my local Public Television station, supposedly objective, used to run daily and repeatedly, an advertisement in which the giant oil company, Chevron, promotes itself under the slogan of "The Power of Human Energy." A moment's thought reveals that Chevron's interest is in energy from oil, not human energy. Chevron is devoted to getting as much money as it can (billions and billions of dollars a year) by extracting fossil fuels out of the earth and thereby contributing big time to global warming. The advertisement is a lie. Learning how to read literature "rhetorically" is primary training in how to spot such lies and distortions.

This is so partly because so much literature deals thematically with imaginary characters who are wrong in their readings of others, for example Elizabeth Bennett in her misreading of Darcy in Jane Austen's *Pride and Prejudice* or Dorothea Brooke's misreading of Edward Casaubon in George Eliot's *Middlemarch*, or Isabel Archer's misreading of Gilbert Osmond in Henry James's *The Portrait of a Lady*. Literature is also training in resisting lies and distortions in the skill it gives in understanding the way the rhetoric of tropes and the rhetoric of persuasion works. Such expertise as literary study gives might be translated to a savvy resistance to the lies and ideological distortions politicians and talk show hosts promulgate, for example the lies of those who deny climate change or the lying claims, believed in by high percentages of Americans, that Barack Obama is a Muslim, a socialist, and not a legitimate president because he was not born in the United States. The motto for this defense of literary study might be the challenging and provocative claim made by Paul de Man in "The Resistance to Theory." "What we call ideology," says de Man, "is precisely the confusion of linguistic with natural reality, of reference with phenomenalism. It follows that, more than any other mode of inquiry, including economics, the linguistics of literariness is a powerful and indispensable tool in the unmasking of ideological aberrations, as well as a determining factor in accounting for their occurrence."[13]

The chances that literary study would have this benign effect on many people are slim. One can only have the audacity of hope and believe that some people who study literature and literary theory might be led to the habit of unmasking ideological aberrations such as those that surround us on all sides in the United States today. The chances are slim because of the difficulty of transferring what you might learn by a careful reading, say, of *The Portrait of a Lady* to unmasking the dominant ideologies that mean a thoughtful person should only vote Republican if her or his income happens to be in the top two per cent of all Americans and if maximizing your wealth in the short term is your only goal. Another great difficulty is the actual situation in American universities today, as I have described it. Derrida's *The University Without Condition* was not exactly greeted with shouts of joyful assent when he presented it as a lecture at Stanford. In spite of their lip-service to teaching so-called "critical thinking," the politicians and corporate executives who preside today over both public and private American colleges and universities are unlikely to support something that would put in question the assumptions on the basis of which they make decisions about who teaches what. They need colleges and universities these days, if at all, primarily to teach math and science, technology, engineering, computer science, basic English composition, and other skills necessary for working in a technologized capitalist economy. The ability to do a rhetorical reading of *Pride and Prejudice* and transfer that skill to politicians' and advertisers' lies is not one of those necessities. I have never yet heard President Barack Obama so much as mention literary study in his eloquent speeches about the urgent need to improve education in the United States.

Notes

1. Jacques Derrida, *L'Université sans condition*. Paris: Galilée, 2001; *ibid.*, "The University Without Condition." Trans. Peggy Kamuf. In *Without Alibi*, ed. and trans. Peggy Kamuf (Stanford, Calif.: Stanford University Press, 2002), 202-37.

2. Peggy Kamuf, "Counting Madness," in *The Future of the Humanities: U.S. Domination and Other Issues*, a special issue of *The Oxford Literary Review*, ed. Timothy Clark and Nicholas Royle, vol. 28 (2006), 67-77.

3. Quoted in Frank Donoghue, "Prestige," *Profession 2006* (New York: The Modern Language Association of America, 2006), 156.

4. http://opa.yale.edu/president/message.aspx?id=91 (Accessed Sept. 6, 2010.)

5. According to Donoghue, "between 1970 and 2001, Bachelor's degrees in English have declined from 7.6 percent to 4 percent, as have degrees in foreign languages (2.4 percent to 1 percent)," *The Last Professors*, 91.

6. Cited in Donoghue, 20.

7. http://www.poemhunter.com/poem/on-sitting-down-to-read-king-lear-once-again/ (Accessed September 6, 2010.)

8. *The Letters of Matthew Arnold to Arthur Hugh Clough*, ed. Howard Foster Lowry (London and New York: Oxford University Press, 1932), 96.

9. For a proposal for such courses see David Pogue's interview of John Palfrey, Harvard Law School professor and co-director of Harvard's Berkman Center for Internet & Society at http://www.nytimes.com/indexes/2010/07/22/technology/personaltechemail/index.html (Accessed September 6, 2010.)

10. W. B. Yeats, *The Variorum Edition of the Poems*, ed. Peter Allt and Russell K. Alspach (New York: Macmillan, 1977), 316.

11. J. Hillis Miller, "W. B. Yeats: 'The Cold Heaven,'" in *Others* (Princeton: Princeton University Press, 2001), 170-182.

12. A. Norman Jeffares, *A Commentary on the Collected Poems of W. B. Yeats* (Stanford, California: Stanford University Press, 1968), 146.

13. Paul de Man, "The Resistance to Theory," in *The Resistance to Theory* (Minneapolis: University of Minnesota Press, 1986), 11.

II

Should We Read Literature Now, and, If So, How? Transgressing Boundaries with Iser and Coetzee

Knocking on the Door of the Past

It is a great honor to be asked to give a Wolfgang Iser Lecture at the University of Konstanz. Wolfgang and I were good friends for many years. He and his wife Lore were exceedingly kind to me and to my wife over those years. It is a great sadness for me that they are gone. When I think of the way our lives intersected, in a kind of transgressing of boundaries, I feel a little as Henry James says he felt when preparing to write down, in *A Small Boy and Others*, his early memories, with a focus on his brother William. "[A]spects began to multiply and images to swarm," writes James, "so far at least as they showed, to appreciation, as true terms and happy values; and that I might positively and exceedingly rejoice in my relation to most of them, using it for all that, as the phrase is, it should be worth. To knock at the door of the past was in a word to see it open to me quite wide—to see the world within begin to 'compose' with a grace of its own round the primary figure, see it people itself vividly and insistently" (2). Though I cannot match James's grandiose eloquence in recording the swarming memories of his childhood, still I can say that I do "positively and exceedingly rejoice" in my many recollections of Wolfgang Iser. They do organize themselves around him as "primary figure." I have the strong sense that over all those years I received from him more than I gave, in more ways than one.

As far as I can remember (though my memory may have "gaps," to use an Iserian word), my first face to face encounter with Wolfgang Iser was at a meeting of the English Institute at Columbia University in 1970. The English Institute was, and still is, an annual meeting of about 150 scholars (perhaps more nowadays), primarily professors of English at that time, to hear papers organized in panels. The English Institute, by the way, moved a good many years ago from Columbia to Harvard. I had asked Paul de Man, then my colleague at Johns Hopkins, to organize a panel on narrative theory for a Columbia meeting of the English Institute. He invited Edward Said, Martin Price, Gérard Genette, and Wolfgang Iser to present papers. Iser gave a paper on filling the gaps in acts of interpretation, "Indeterminacy and the Reader's Response in Prose Fiction."[1] This was, I believe, Iser's first major public appearance in the United States.

What I remember most about that meeting, along with hearing Iser's lecture, was coming upon Iser and de Man in earnest conversation in the hall outside the auditorium after Iser's paper had been delivered. De Man was (unsuccessfully) trying to persuade Iser that the gaps are inside the words, not between them. Much is at stake in that difference. It was the irresistible force meeting the immovable rock. Iser just looked skeptical and would not budge.

Iser's work changed over the years, all right, but at his own pace and in unpredictable ways under unpredictable influences. An example is his late turn to anthropology proper, not just literary anthropology. This is exemplified in the influence on that late work of Eric Gans's writings, as well as of work by Claude Levi-Strauss, André Leroi-Gourhan, and other anthropologists, many of whom are mentioned in the preface to *The Fictive and the Imaginary*.[2] Iser says, however, that these anthropologists, even Gans, are to unable to account for the role of the fictive in human and social life. In his late work Iser no longer focused on explaining how the reader's response to a literary text fills in gaps and makes a meaningful *Gestalt* out of to some degree indeterminate signs. He now became most interested in trying to explain the human and social function of literature. He wanted to understand how it is that "art appears to be indispensable, because it is a means of human self-exegesis," that is, how it is that "literature seems to be necessary as a continual patterning of human plasticity" (FIe, xiii).

Sometime after our first meeting, I encouraged Iser to publish the English translation of *Der implizite Leser* with the Johns Hopkins Press. He translated it himself. He told me that doing that had been immensely hard work, almost like writing a new book. He had found by experience that German academic prose does not always make good sense when translated more or less literally into English. "You just cannot say it that way in English," he discovered. It is true that the conventions of academic writing differ markedly in the two countries and in the two languages. In the United States we are encouraged to write as much as possible in idiomatic English that anyone can understand. German academic lingo is, or was, almost a separate language, in Iser's hands at least. It was an idiom with its own rules and protocols. The magisterial *Poetik und Hermeneutik* series of collected essays and discussions, one of the great achievements of the Konstanz School, is all written, more or less, in that idiom. I remember that Paul de Man, who taught one summer at Konstanz, while I was teaching in Zürich, and who attended one of the *Poetik und Hermeutik* conferences (papers, discussions, and all), reported to me, "You won't believe this, but they actually can talk in the same style in which they write." Iser's *Das Fiktive und das Imaginäre*, my focus in this essay, was originally a contribution to the work of a *Poetik und Hermeneutic* project on *Konstitution und Funktion fiktionaler Texte*. The translation of *Das Fiktive und das Imaginäre*, by the way, I have discovered by checking my citations back and forth, does not always correspond at all literally to what the German says. Iser approved and revised the translation, so I suppose he could allow himself latitude in turning his German into English. Even the subtitle was significantly changed. "Charting Literary Anthropology" does not have at all the same nuance as "Perspektiven literarischer Anthropologie."

Over the years Iser and I had many professional contacts, mostly through his kindness in inviting me a number of times to lecture at Konstanz. In the case of a series of lectures I gave there for the *Konstanzer Dialoge,* Iser very generously arranged the translation into German of the book that developed from those lectures, *Illustration* (Harvard and Reaktion Books, 1992). The German version (Universitätsverlag Konstanz, 1993, translated by Monika Reif-Hülser) starts with a perceptive survey by Iser himself of all my work until then. He, or someone at Konstanz, also added a resonant German subtitle, not in the English version: "Die Spur der Zeichen in Kunst, Kritik und Kultur." "Die Spur der Zeichen": I would never have thought of that! Nor of using as cover illustration an admirable Edward Gorey etching of a man climbing a hill in a thunderstorm, no doubt following the trace of the sign.

A final professional note: When I was considering the move from Yale to the University of California at Irvine, Iser, who had already been teaching for a number of years as a permanently appointed intermittent visiting professor at Irvine, called me by phone at Yale and told me persuasively all the reasons why I should move to Irvine. That call was important in tipping the balance toward my decision to join the Irvine faculty. There I happily had Wolfgang Iser as a colleague and friend for a good many years. His Irvine connection was shadowed in the last years of it by the new absurdly onerous United States visa regulations that required him to go to Frankfurt and be at the American embassy standing in line at five in the morning to fill out endless forms that included weird questions like, "What was the name of your high school principal?" I do not blame Iser for beginning to wonder if it was worth it, much as he valued his Irvine teaching. Those post 9/11 visa rules have greatly damaged American international academic exchanges for visiting professors and conference attendees in all fields, not to speak of the admission of graduate students from outside the United States.

What I remember most, however, when I knock on the door of memory and the recollections of Wolfgang Iser come tumbling out, is the many meals and outings we had together over the years. On my first visit to lecture at Konstanz, he met my plane in Zürich and drove me back to Konstanz in what I remember as a very big and very fast Mercedes. His general idea was that oncoming cars on the then narrow road would be sure to get out of our way, which they did. He was a conspicuously expert driver. On another occasion he took me on a tour of wineries near Konstanz. I remember especially one in a monastery. On yet another occasion when I was lecturing in Konstanz he took me on successive nights to eat venison at three different restaurants: in Germany, Austria, and Switzerland.

At Irvine we had the custom, during his visits there, always to go with our wives on some outing or other. On one occasion, for example, we stayed over a weekend in a resort hotel in the Anza Borrego desert. Iser always drove on those occasions, in his large rented car. Finally, I remember with great pleasure our dinners to celebrate my March 5 birthday at

Gustav Anders, a Swedish restaurant in Irvine that met Iser's stringent standards. Those standards meant good service in a pleasant ambience, good very dry white wine and good beef steaks unadorned with sauce. Never mind the vegetables. That restaurant has, alas, vanished, its owner back in Sweden, as has that epoch of the flourishing of theory at Irvine. In that happy time not only Iser, but also Jacques Derrida, Jean-François Lyotard, and other theorists taught regularly at Irvine under the benign leadership of Murray Krieger.

Lest my recollections seem unduly centered on gourmandise, let me celebrate in conclusion Wolfgang's deep knowledge of music, to which I owe much. I recall in particular going with the Isers to a great performance of *Die Meistersinger* in Munich, the whole five or more hours of it, with a break for dinner; the Isers' spectacular collection of CDs in their Konstanz home; and the occasion on which he told me just which recording of Bach's *Christmas Oratorio* to buy and just which shop in Munich to buy it in when I was making another visit to Munich shortly before Christmas. The Isers' love of Vienna, in considerable part for the great concerts there, is one sadness of Wolfgang's death and of Lore's subsequent passing.

Is The Fictive and the Imaginary *a Fictive Work?*

I turn now to account briefly as best I can for the chief features of Wolfgang Iser's thinking about literature.[3] That thinking is an indispensable and quite unique contribution to the late twentieth-century epochal efflorescence of literary theory and literary criticism. Iser's writing is not like anyone else's. To give a full accounting of Iser's work as a literary scholar in its permutations over the years from reader response theory to literary anthropology is well beyond the scope of a single lecture. It is perhaps beyond my powers generally, however much space and time I were given. I want to attempt something much more modest: to read the preface and first chapter of his book of 1991, called, in translation, *The Fictive and the Imaginary* (1993). That first chapter is called, in English, "Fictionalizing Acts," in German "Akte des Fingierens." I choose this twenty-page chapter somewhat arbitrarily, partly because it exemplifies so well Iser's turn in his later work to what he called "literary anthropology," partly for the somewhat sentimental reason that *The Fictive and the Imaginary* more or less coincides in date with my lectures in Konstanz, sponsored by Iser, on *Illustration*, that is, more broadly, on *ekphrasis*. I will then in conclusion try to see whether Iser's "literary anthropology" helps us to understand and make use today of J. M. Coetzee's *Waiting for the Barbarians*. Doing that might hint at an answer to my title question, "Should we read literature now, and, if so, how?" How should we read *Waiting for the Barbarians* now? What good is it in these bad days to read it at all?

I must begin by confessing that I do not find Iser's opening chapter, "Fictionalizing Acts," all that easy to grasp. I have read it over and over. I still feel it to some degree eludes my attempt to possess it. Perhaps that may be because those German conventions for academic discourse were carried over to some degree by the various translators who collaborated in the work of Übersetzung: David Henry Wilson, John Paul Riquelme, and Emily Budick, along with Iser himself as the final arbiter. Conceptual words in German can never be translated into English in a fully satisfactory way. Each carries the freight of the long history of its usage in German. An example would be Iser's use of the word "intentionality." This word must be understood in its Husserlian context, a context most likely unknown to many readers of the English translation. In spite of those contexts, Iser's discourse is to a considerable degree sui generis. I know no other theorist whose discourse sounds at all like his. In my attempt to explain what Iser says, I shall follow through his textual labyrinth the Ariadne's thread of my initial question: Is "Fictionalizing Acts" itself fictive, by Iser's definition of fictive?

That question seems on the face of it absurd. Iser's discourse, so it seems, is not fictive at all. It is a sober, reasoned attempt to define the fictive and its role in human life. Iser's tools for doing that are a multitude of abstract conceptual terms: the real, the fictive, the imaginary, "the text," transgression, act, intentionality, selection, combination, event, background, "derestriction," play, and so on, in ever-expanding multiplicity. Iser's text is composed of the permutation and combination of these terms as the entities they name are dynamically interrelated around the goal of defining the fictive.

A good bit of the difficulty, for me at least, of understanding just what Iser is saying is that his writing remains at a high level of complex manipulation of conceptual abstractions, even though he tirelessly explains just what he means by a given term, for example, "selection." The explanations, however, involve more abstractions, with only a minimum of concrete exemplifications. Here, in case you have not read Iser lately, is one example of the pervasive stylistic texture of Iser's discourse: "Thus what is absent is made present. But while the realized combination draws its life from what it has excluded, the fictionalizing act of relating clearly brings about a copresence of the realized and the absent. This in turn causes the realized relations to be undermined. It makes them sink back into the shadows of background existence, so that new relations can come to the fore, gaining stability against this background." ("... dadurch kommt das Abwesende zur Gegenwart. Lebt aber die realisierte Beziehung von dem, was sie abweist, so bringt de Relationierung als Produkt eines fingierenden Aktes das Realisierte und das Absesende prinzipiell in eine Ko-Präsenz, die bewirkt, daß realisierte Beziehungen in ihre Schattenhaftigkeit zurückfallen und andere sich vor ihnen zu stabilisieren vermögen.") (FIe, 8; FIg, 29-30)

Iser's instinct, as you can see, or perhaps his deliberate strategy, is to begin at the top, so to speak, where he has the widest perspective, rather than with the nitty-gritty of specific examples to be accounted for. The latter starting place would be my own penchant. Though Iser recognizes more than once in "Fictionalizing Acts" that any given fiction is in various ways embedded in history, he wants, like many other philosophers and theorists, to make statements of all-inclusive generality, statements about what the fictive is and what it does that are good for all times, for all places, and for all cultures.

In my attempt to account for Iser's discourse, I may be helped by remembering Walter Benjamin's distinction, in "The Task of the Translator," between *das Gemeinte*, what is meant, and *die Art des Meinens*, the way meaning is expressed. Paul de Man, in his essay on Benjamin's essay, calls the study of *das Gemeinte* "hermeneutics" and the study of *die Art des Meinens* "poetics." That terminology is probably a covert reference to Konstanz School *Hermeneutics and Poetics*. One is," says de Man, "so attracted by problems of meaning that it is impossible to do hermeneutics and poetics at the same time. From the moment you start to get involved with problems of meaning, as I unfortunately tend to do, forget about the poetics. The two are not complementary, the two may be mutually exclusive in a certain way...."[4] One can only hope de Man is wrong, since a lot is at stake in what he says, though I fear he may be right.

It is easy enough, after some repeated close readings, to identify schematically what Iser means in "Fictionalizing Acts," what his *Gemeinte* is. As opposed to the long tradition, with its many permutations going back to Aristotelian *mimesis*, defining the fictive more or less exclusively in terms of its oppositional or dialectical relation to the real, Iser asserts that a third term, "the imaginary," must be invoked. The imaginary "is basically a featureless and inactive potential" (FIe, xvii; not present in the German "Vorwort") in human beings for dreams, "fantasies, projections, daydreams, and other reveries" ("Phantasmen, Projektionen und Tagträumen") (FIe, 3; FIg, 21), as well as for activating fictions. The imaginary is, in a phrase not translated into the English version, "diffus, formlos, unfixiert und ohne Objektreferenz" (FIg, 21): diffuse, formless, unfixed, and without objective reference. Iser's imaginary must not be thought of as in any way a transcendent entity, a divine realm of potential forms. Iser's thinking is resolutely a-religious, anti-idealist. The imaginary is an exclusively human potential. Nor are the real, the fictive, or the imaginary thought of by Iser as purely linguistic entities. Though he recognizes that literary texts, as embodiments of the fictive, are made of words, and though he talks a lot about "semantics," Iser appears to have a prejudice against language-based literary theories. "Whoever wants to understand language must understand more than just language" ("wer Sprache verstehen will, mehr als nur Sprache verstehen muß") says Iser firmly (FIe,18; FIg, 46). That sounds plausible enough, but it tends to lead him, nevertheless, to downplay the constitutive role of language in generating fictions. He says, for example: "Every literary text inevitably contains a selection from a variety of social, historical, cultural, and literary systems that exist as referential fields outside the text." ("Daraus ergibt sich die für jeden fiktionalen Text notwendige *Selektion* aus den vorhandenen Umweltsystemen, seien diese sozio-kultureller Natur oder solche der Literatur selbst.") (FIe, 4; FIg, 24) The literary text, however, it is easy to see, does not contain items from those systems as such, but rather the names for them, as Iser's phrase "referential fields" does, after all, imply.

Iser in the German original calls these referential fields the "Umweltsystemen," a word not easily translated into English. This amalgamation, however, does not simply provide new perspectives on the real. "Reality, then," says Iser, "may be reproduced in a fictional text, but it is there in order to be outstripped, as is indicated by its being bracketed." ("So wird zwar Wirklichkeit im fiktionalen Text wiederholt, doch durch die Einklammerung wird ihr Wiederholtwerden überragt.") (FIe, 13; FIg, 38) The essential function of the fictive "as if" is to give form to the diffuseness of the imaginary: "Our subsequent journey to new horizons translates the imaginary into an experience—an experience that is shaped by the degree of determinacy given to the imaginary by the fictional 'as-if.'" ("Durch diese Ereignishaftigkeit übersetz sich das Imagináäre in eine Erfahrung. Ermöglicht wird diese durch den Grad der Bestimmtheit, den das Imaginäre durch den Modus des Als-Ob gewinnt.") (FIe, 17; FIg, 45) The literary text is "a pragmatization of the imaginary" ("die Pragmatisierung des Imaginären") (FIe, 18; FIg, 46). The "matrix" of the literary text is not the real and not fictive language, but "the multiplicitous availability of the imaginary" ("die multiple Verfügbarket des Imaginären") (FIe, 19; FIg, 48). In giving pragmatic form to the formless imaginary, the fictive "outstrips" language. Here is another example of Iser's suspicion of language-based theories: "Thus the cardinal points of the text defy verbalization (entziehen sich . . . der Versprachlichung)," says Iser in the final sentences of "Fictionalizing Acts," "and it is only through these open structures within the linguistic patterning of the text that the imaginary can manifest its presence. From this fact we can deduce one last achievement of the fictive in the fictional text: It brings about the presence of the imaginary by transgressing language itself (als die Sprache selbst überschritten). In outstripping (in solcher Hintergehbarkeit) what conditions it, the imaginary reveals itself as the generative matrix of the text (als den Ermöglichungsgrund des Textes)" (FIe, 20-21; FIg, 51).

This all makes perfect sense. It is a magnificently persuasive and original theory of fiction, one that, so far as I know, has no parallels either in work by other scholars today or in the long Western tradition of wrestling to define the fictive as-if. One last question from the realm of *das Gemeinte*: Just what human good is achieved by the fictive? Why do human beings need fictions? Iser's answer is unequivocal. Though the fictive may give us new critical perspectives on the real, and be a pleasure in itselkf, its most important function is to expand the number of "pragmatizations" of that basic human plasticity Iser calls the imaginary. That human beings are essentially to be defined by their plasticity is Iser's fundamental anthropological assumption. "If the plasticity of human nature allows," he avers in the "Preface," "through its multiple culture-bound patternings, limitless human self-cultivation, literature becomes a panorama of what is possible, because it is not hedged in by either the limitations or the considerations that determine the institutionalized organizations within which human life otherwise takes its course" (FIe, xviii-xix; not in the German "Vorwort"). Fulfilling as many as possible of the limitless ways to be human is a good in itself. Using fictionalizing acts as a means of giving form to the formless plasticity of the imaginary is the best way to do that. This gives one answer to the question in my title. We should read literature now and at any other time because doing so is the best form of limitless human self-cultivation. How should we read literature? By opening ourselves to the imaginary worlds literary works make available.

⚘

My sketching out of Iser's *Gemeinte* in "Fictionalizing Acts" seems to confirm that it is through and through a closely reasoned argument. It is a discourse not in any sense fictive. If I turn for a close look at Iser's *Art des Meinens*, as opposed to *das Gemeinte*, in his chapter, however, something quite different begins to appear. It seems to come out from the shadowy background into the bright foreground, to use one of Iser's own figures. To bring Iser's art of meaning into focus might entail highlighting the austere impersonality of his discourse. It scrupulously avoids any self-reference, any admission that a particular scholar in a particular situation is making up these words and setting them down on paper. Iser's words seem to be spoken by a disembodied truth-speaker. That is part of their force. Another feature of Iser's *Art des Meinens* is the casual brief illustrative citations from a wide and heterogeneous variety of authorities, Nelson Goodman side by side with Husserl side by side with Vaihinger, and so on. These citations are made part of Iser's argument, just as, according to Iser, makers of fictions appropriate elements from the world-systems of the real socio-political and cultural worlds to fabricate their pragmatizations of the imaginary. Such heterogeneous references give Iser's discourse authority by implying that he has read more or less everything and can call up apposite citations and references with effortless learning. Identification of Iser's art of meaning might, finally, want to describe how Iser's rhetoric of presentation proceeds logically from the real to the fictive to the imaginary. He develops his argument by stages to show how these elements are dynamically interrelated. His act of exposition matches the procedure of the "fictionalizing acts" he is describing.

All these rhetorical procedures are features of Iser's *Art des Meinens*, as opposed to his *Gemeinte*, what he means to say. I want to empasize most, however, a feature of Iser's discourse that has been shadowily present in my citations but that I have not yet brought to the fore. This is the constant use of overt or covert spatial figures of speech. These collaborate to create in the reader, in me as reader at least, though my response may be idiosyncratic, a distinct imaginary space visible to my mind's eye. In this strange intellectual landscape, the real is somewhere off to the left, the fictive is in the middle at my focus of attention, and the imaginary is off to the right as a somewhat blurred and diffuse cloud of visible invisibility that is nevertheless the generative matrix, "der Ermöglichungsgrund," of all fictionalizing acts. This mental landscape is peopled by animated abstractions engaged in lively dynamic and mutually defining interaction with one another. Elements from the real are selected, combined, and self-disclosed in order to give form to the formless imaginary and to expand once more through a new embodiment human beings' infinite plasticity. One can see why Iser tends to downplay language, since it is these ever-changing spatial *Gestalts* and their elements that most interest him, not the role of language in creating them. One can also see why he instinctively wants to efface his own or any author's invention of this dance of abstractions. He wants to imply that these fictionalizing acts take place as it were of their own accord, not through his invention, nor through the choices of any particular authors of fictions. They are acts to a large degree without actors.

"Fictionalizing Acts" abounds in spatial terms that implicitly coach the reader to create the imaginary space I am describing. These spring into visibility once you shift your attention from meaning to the means of making meaning, from hermeneutics to poetics. The passage I began by citing as an example of Iser's style is a splendid example of this spatial imagination: "This in turn causes the realized relations to be undermined. It makes them sink back into the shadows of background existence, so that new relations can come to the fore, gaining stability against this background." Iser speaks of the way external social systems "move into focus and can be discerned as the referential fields of the text" ("Zunächst rücken die Bezugsfelder als solche in den Blick") (FIe, 5; FIg, 24). This spatial word "field" recurs frequently, as in the following: "Through the relational process (die Relationierung) fields of reference (Bezugsfelder) had to be produced from the material selected [note that he does not say, "from the material the *author* selected"], and these fields, in turn, had to be linked with each other (der Relationierung dieser Felden untereinander), thereby becoming subjected to a reciprocal transformation" (FIe,11; FIg, 34). "Relation" here becomes a spatial term, a matter of "linking" in the English translation, as animals may be linked together with a rope, or as a chain is made of "links." The sentence also exemplifies what I mean by dynamic interaction, that constant movement of elements in what I am calling a dance or agon of embodied abstractions, as foreground fades and background emerges, as in a passage already cited (FIe, 8; FIg, 29-30), "Bracketing" ("Einklammerung") (FIe, 13; FIg, 38), "open-ended" ("die Offenheit") (FIe, 20; FIg, 51), "patternings" (FIe, xviii; not in the German "Vorwort"), "cardinal points" ("die archimedischen Punkte") (FIe, 20; FIg, 51; the German here has a quite different meaning from "cardinal points"), "generative matrix" ("Konstitutionsgrund," "Ermöglichungsgrund") (FIe, 18, 21; FIg, 46, 51), "gestalt" (FIe, 3; FIg, 21), "semantic topography" ("semantische Topographie") (FIe,10; FIg, 32), and many other apparently conceptual terms in Iser's discourse covertly encourage the reader to think of a spatial field in constant "kaleidoscopic" (FIe, xviii; not in the German "Vorwort") transformation.

The most important and most frequently recurring spatial terms, however, in Iser's *Art des Meinens,* are phrases like "transgressing boundaries," "crossing borders," "overstepping," and the like. Too many of these exist to be cited in this essay, but here are a few: "The act of fictionalizing is a crossing of boundaries (Grenzüberschreitung). It amounts to nothing short of an act of transgression. This transgressive function of the fictionalizing act links it to the imaginary" (FIe, 3; FIg 21; calling it "an act of transgression" is added in the translation, though it is one translation used by Iser for "Überschreitung"). "This selection is itself a stepping beyond boundaries (Grenzüberschreitung)" (FIe, 4; FIg, 24). "Combination, too, is an act of fictionalizing, with the same basic mode of operation: the crossing of boundaries (Grenzüberschreitung)" (FIe, 7; FIg, 27). "Reality, then, may be reproduced in a fictional text, but it is there in order to be outstripped (überragt), as is indicated by its being bracketed" (FIe, 13; FIg, 38). "Once again boundaries are overstepped (eine zweifache Grenzüberschretung): the world of the text is exceeded and the diffuseness of the imaginary assumes form" (FIe,16; FIg, 43; the translation deviates a bit from the German here, as in many other places). In the light of this salient spatializing motif, we can see in a new *Art des Meinens* perspective a passage at the end of the chapter already cited for its conceptual meaning. The fictive, says Iser in that passage, "brings about the presence of the imaginary by transgressing language itself. In outstripping what conditions it, the imaginary reveals itself as the generative matrix of the text" (FIe, 21; FIg, 51).

All this somewhat lurid talk about transgressing boundaries is not, in my judgment, inherent in the purely conceptual argument Iser is making. It surprised me when I first read the essay. It seemed unnecessarily melodramatic as a description of the relatively harmless operations being described. These recurrent figures of transgressing or overstepping borders delineate the imaginary field generated in the reader by Iser's text as a place of rigidly enforced boundaries between the real, the fictive, and the imaginary and between the elements that are selected for combination to produce the fictive as a pragmatization of the imaginary. "Transgressing" is a strong word. It suggests that the continual crossing of borders in this dance or battle of embodied abstractions is a violent and illicit act, something like sneaking across a border without a proper passport or visa. The entities that transgress boundaries become illegal aliens in the new country, something "from away" as they say on my adopted home island, Deer Isle, Maine. Those "from here" use "from away" as an epithet for anyone who was not born on Deer Isle and whose ancestors for many generations were not born there too. The border-crossings Iser describes may be a good thing, since they allow the use of the fictive as new ways to give form to human plasticity. Iser's language, however, suggests that doing this nevertheless is a somewhat illicit and dangerous operation. Crossing borders always involves an obscure sense of danger and guilt.

"Fictionalizing Acts" not only stages a complex imaginary space for the reader's spectatorship, a space that is shadowily present behind the conceptual argument. It also tells in that space a covert story of transgressive border crossings, such as I have performed to come here to Konstanz and such as Wolfgang Iser performed in his many visits to the United States. Those border crossings, I might note, also involve a translation from one language region to another, an Übersetzung or Übertragung. I conclude that Iser's *Art des Meinens* does make "Fictionalizing Acts" itself an act of fictionalizing. It does what it talks about. Its great force as a text derives as much from its creation and peopling of an imaginary space as from the originality and cogency of the conceptual argument it makes.

Does that mean that hermeneutics and poetics, *die Art des Meinens* and *das Gemeinte,* can, in an analysis of Iser's chapter such as mine, be happily reconciled, *pace* de Man? I do not think so. Iser's hermeneutic meaning is a cheerful story of expansion through the fictive of human plasticity, whereas attention to his poetics uncovers a quite different story of multiple risky, illicit, transgressive border crossings and translations, "Übersetzungen," settings-over. That story is irreconcilable with the overt meaning a hermeneutic reading might identify.

Transgressing Borders in Coetzee's *Waiting for the Barbarians*

I begin this final section with a question: Does J. M. Coetzee's *Waiting for the Barbarians*[5] confirm or disconfirm Iser's paradigm for the way fictionalizing acts work? The answer is clear. Coetzee's novel spectacularly confirms what Iser says. *Waiting for the Barbarians* selects, combines, and self-discloses elements from "a variety of social, historical, cultural, and literary systems that exist as referential fields outside the text" (Iser's formulation, cited above [FIe, 4; FIg, 24]). In this case, the text is fabricated of elements from what we all know about imperialist conquests over the years, about imperialist ideologies, about the way imperialisms establish frontier outposts at the borders of empires as they pause before invading further, about nomad life, about the use of extralegal torture as an interrogation device by special forces like our CIA or like the police in South Africa under Apartheid, or more recently by United States special forces and their accomplices at Abu Graib and Guantánamo Bay, in Egypt, Pakistan, and who knows where else around the world.

Waiting for the Barbarians was published in 1980, when South Africa was still suffering under Apartheid. It is a novel of poignant political protest, though the facts of life under Apartheid are translated into a fictive empire that has no direct correspondence to South African landscape or social and racial structure. Coetzee also transfers to his novel elements from what we know of human sexuality, of human culinary habits, of army garrisons, of desert landscapes and their weather, of human pain, sickness, and hunger. These elements, along with others that might be specified, for example a reference to the Sigmund Freud essay, "A Child Is being Beaten,"[6] or to the conventions of postmodern realist fiction, are transgressed in the Iserian sense of being transformed and recombined to create an imaginary world that has no specific real life referent and is not a pastiche or parody of other literary works. One cannot read *Waiting for the Barbarians*, however, without thinking of its resonances with Kafka's work, not only, of course, with "In der Strafkolonie" ("In the Penal Colony"), but also with many other features of Kafka stories and novels, for example the motif of ominous waiting in "Der Bau" ("The Burrow"),[7] or Kafkesque motifs such as the virtually uncrossable spatial and social expanses in the group of stories and parables about empires, such as the empire Kafka imagined in "Ein kaiserliche Botschaft" ("An Imperial Message").[8] The imaginary world of *Waiting for the Barbarians* is to some considerable degree "Kafkesque," or at least seems so to me and to many other readers. A reference to Beckett's *Waiting for Godot* may, however, lurk in Coetzee's title. Coetzee's PhD dissertation in linguistics at the University of Texas (1969) was on computer stylistic analysis of Beckett's works. Kafka, Beckett, and Coetzee, all three, dramatize in pragmatizations of the imaginary the real human experience of seemingly interminable waiting. A more recent novel by a Chinese American, Ha Jin's *Waiting*,[9] which Coetzee of course could not have known in 1980, tells the story of an army doctor living in Communist China. He must wait for eighteen years before he can divorce his unloved wife by an arranged marriage and marry the nurse he loves, or thinks he loves. Once that happens, he is still dissatisfied. "Waiting," it seems, has come to define him through and through, as an interminable condition. To put this in Iserian terms, the experience of prolonged, unending waiting is a specific pragmatization of the imaginary. Expressing it textually may transgressively appropriate a selection from an indefinite number of elements in the Weltsystemen.

Waiting for the Barbarians is an expansive pragmatization of human plasticity, that is, its potential for giving form to the imaginary. When I read this novel I am transported into an "as if" world that does not exist except in the words on the page and that is nevertheless described as circumstantially as if it really existed. Though Iser does not stress the narrative aspect of the literary fictive, *Waiting for the Barbarians* also enacts a haunting and troubling story within the fictive mise en scène it generates with the imaginary as mothering matrix.

That story may be briefly told: The aging Magistrate of a frontier oasis on the edge of an Empire, an oasis that lives at peace with the nomads across the border, has his calm life invaded by the army and the special forces of the Third Bureau of the Civil Guard from the Empire's distant capital. These forces periodically make grand marches into the barbarians' territory. These are always totally counter-productive and self-defeating because they are based on ideological misconceptions, somewhat like our assumption that we had to invade Iraq because Saddam Hussein had weapons of mass destruction poised to flatten our homeland cities. The Third Bureau's ideological paranoia about danger from invasion by the nomad barbarians leads them to capture and torture an innocent group of barbarian men, women, and children in the attempt to extract non-existent knowledge from them about the barbarians' non-existent war plans. In a similar way, we tortured prisoners from Iraq who, for the most part, had no knowledge whatsoever about Al Queda terrorist plots, but just happened to be in the wrong place at the wrong time or to have been falsely reported on by their neighbors. After half an hour or so of torture, anyone can be brought to confess to anything, or to make up wild stories to get the pain to stop.

The Magistrate rescues a girl who has been tortured, her ankles broken, her eyes more than half blinded, by the sinister torturer Colonel Joll.

She has been left behind when the tortured prisoners are released to go back to their nomad life. The Magistrate takes the girl into his room. He eventually takes her back to her barbarian countrymen, deep in the desert, when his relation to her fails. The Magistrate is arrested on his return for "treasonously consorting with the enemy" (WB, 90). He escapes his prison more than once, but ultimately returns to arrest. He is himself beaten and then barbarously tortured when he tries to prevent the public beating and torture of some bedraggled prisoners the Third Bureau and the army have brought back from one of their catastrophic forays. It is the Empire that is barbarous, as the Magistrate says. The army and the Third Bureau, what is left of it, after a final disastrous campaign, abandon the settlement and return home, having first looted all the homes and shops in the settlement. The novel ends with the Magistrate returned to his old position of authority in the nearly empty oasis, waiting with the remaining others for the expected invasion and occupation by the barbarians, in a catastrophic end to empire-building, an end has not quite yet happened at the conclusion of the novel. They are left "waiting for the barbarians." The truly barbarous Empire has brought about what it at first falsely imagined as imminent danger from the "barbarian" nomads.

Well, so what? What is the point of this particular story, beyond its successful creation of a not entirely pleasant, in fact deeply disturbing, "pragmatization" of the imaginary and its powerful indirect indictment of Apartheid? To answer these questions I need to go beyond what Iser says in "Fictionalizing Acts." Iser's account remains at a level of generality intended to apply to all examples of the fictive. He wants to indicate, as I have said, the way all examples of the making concrete of the imaginary are goods in themselves. But surely a given example of the giving body to the disembodied imaginary has specific qualities and specific uses, as Iser's lengthy account of the pastoral tradition in Chapter Two of *The Fictive and the Imaginary* persuasively demonstrates. My going beyond Iser, which is a transgression of my own, would involve both *das Gemeinte*, the meaning of *Waiting for the Barbarians*, and *die Art des Meinens*, the way the story is told.

As for the art of making meaning, I would need to account for the frequent explicit descriptions of sex in *Waiting for the Barbarians*. Are they no more than what is expected in a postmodern novel, or do they have some function? I would also need to account for three somewhat strange narratological strategies: 1) *Waiting for the Barbarians* is told in the first person, from inside the Magistrate's mind, feelings, and bodily sensations. I suppose that is because Coetzee's focus is on what happens to the Magistrate, but why not tell that in a third person narration, so some narrator's comment on the Magistrate could be included? 2) The story uses the present tense from beginning to end. This is highly unusual in Western fictions. The third person anonymous narrator of Dickens's *Bleak House* uses the present tense, though the other half of that novel's narration, Esther Summerson's first person story, is in the conventional past tense. I suppose Coetzee employs the present tense to give the novel the appearance of happening in an endless inescapable present, the presence or non-presence of the Magistrate's consciousness to itself, but it is still a little-used narrative technique. It seems odd, in need of explanation, like the choice of first person narration. 3) The story is punctuated by the recounting of many dreams the Magistrate has. These are, so to speak, imaginaries within the primary imaginary. I suppose they function to support the illusion of reality in the primary imaginary realm, but also at the same time to lead the reader to see that the primary level also has the quality of a dream, as all fictive acts to some degree do.

To account for *das Gemeinte* in *Waiting for the Barbarians*, I would need to shift from the meaning of the story to the question of the performative effect on the reader of taking in that meaning. Iser speaks infrequently of this turn back of the imaginary to have effects in the real world, though he does allow for it, as when he observes that the political element in Virgil's *Eclogues* is "the means of righting something that threatens to go wrong" ("die Heilung dessen, was sich zur Gefährdung auszuwachsen droht") (FIe, 34; FIg, 75). *Waiting for the Barbarians* is a courageous indictment of imperialist ideology and behavior at any time, and of recent ones in particular, such as Coetzee's experience at the time he was writing the novel of Apartheid in South Africa, or such as the comparisons with the United States' recent behavior I have been irresistibly led to make. As a more detailed reading would show, this indictment in *Waiting for the Barbarians* takes the form of vividly imagining the experiences of two fictive victims of torture, the barbarian girl and the Magistrate himself. The imperialists and their torturing functionaries, as

I have said, are the true barbarians. The Magistrate says this in so many words when he denounces the master-torturer, Colonel Joll: "'Those pitiable prisoners you brought in—are *they* the enemy I must fear? Is that what you say? *You* are the enemy, Colonel!' I can restrain myself no longer. I pound the desk with my fist. '*You* are the enemy, *you* have made the war, and *you* have given them all the martyrs they need—starting not now but a year ago when you committed your first filthy barbarities here! History will bear me out!'" (WB, 131).

The Magistrate poses two questions: How can torturers come to be? How they can bear to live with themselves? He puts these questions directly to Mandel, the Third Bureau officer who has tortured him: "Do not misunderstand me. I am not blaming you or accusing you. I am long past that. Remember, I too have devoted a life to the law, I know its processes, I know that the workings of justice are often obscure. I am only trying to understand. I am trying to understand the zone in which you live. I am trying to understand how you breathe and eat and live from day to day. But I cannot! That is what troubles me! If I were he, I say to myself, my hands would feel so dirty that it would choke me—" (WB, 145-6). Upon which Mandel hits him hard in the chest, and shouts, "You bastard! . . . You fucking old lunatic! Get out! Go and die somewhere!" (WB, 146).

This would seem to give a clear answer to the uses of *Waiting for the Barbarians*. Writing with disturbing prophetic power in 1980, on the basis of his experience at the time of Apartheid, but long before 9/11 (2001), our invasion of Afghanistan (2001) and Iraq (2003), and the torture of prisoners at Abu Graib (2004) and at Guantánamo Bay thereafter, Coetzee anticipated what those events would be like and are still like. I call seeing these uncanny foreshadowings or premonitions by the name "anachronistic reading."[10] Reading *Waiting for the Barbarians* now, with close attention to its details and with thoughtful consideration of its contemporary relevance might (or might not) change not just our attitudes, but even our behavior. I stress "close attention to its details." The meaning and the art of meaning are both in the details.

A further complexity arises, however, from attention to the detail of *die Art des Meinens* in *Waiting for the Barbarians*, something that makes it difficult just to deplore what our army and its torturers have done as something we would never have done ourselves. *Waiting for the Barbarians* implicates the Magistrate in the barbaric injustices he condemns, just as all Americans are complicit in our recent wars of conquest, at the very least by voting and paying taxes, as well as in other ways, for example by secretly enjoying horrible news photos of torture in Abu Graib or of dead and maimed civilians as a result of our bombings. The Magistrate's share in the Empire's guilt is partly by way of his complicity, whether he wishes it or not, as a Magistrate of a border settlement of the Empire, in its barbaric behavior: "For I was not, as I liked to think, the indulgent pleasure-loving opposite of the cold rigid Colonel. I was the lie that the Empire tells itself when times are easy, he the truth that Empire tells when harsh winds blow" (WB, 156). More subtly, and more as a result of the way meaning is expressed in this novel than as an explicitly expressed meaning, a not so covert equation is made between sexual conquest and political conquest by torture. That equation is the basic tropological transfer on which Coetzee's art of meaning rests. "The crime that is latent in ourselves we must inflict on ourselves" (WB, 170), as the Magistrate tells Colonel Joll, mouthing the words through the locked window of Joll's carriage as he flees the settlement after his last calamitous invasion of the barbarian's land.

The torturer tries, unsuccessfully, to penetrate into the most secret recesses of his victims by inflicting extreme pain and humiliation. The male lover, such as the Magistrate, tries, unsuccessfully, to penetrate into the secret recesses of the beloved by making love to her. In both cases the discovery is that the other person remains implacably other. *Waiting for the Barbarians* is, among other things, the story of a distressingly unsuccessful love affair. The Magistrate tries to make up for what has been done to the barbarian girl by taking her to his bed, by pitying her, loving her, trying to heal her wounded feet and ankles by rubbing them and her whole body with oil,[11] caressing her naked body, and ultimately, on the way through the desert to return her to her barbarian kinsmen, by actually making love to her for the first time. None of this works as compensation or as penetrative intersubjective understanding, any more than the Magistrate's pathetic resistance to the Empire's injustices works. The barbarian girl remains as detached and as indifferent as ever. "To desire her has meant to enfold her and enter her, to pierce her surface and stir the quiet of her interior into an ecstatic storm; then to retreat, to subside, to wait for desire to reconstitute itself. But with this woman it is as if there is no interior, only a surface across which I hunt back and forth seeking entry. Is this how her torturers felt hunting their secret, whatever they thought it was?" (WB, 49) The barbarian girl decides, when the Magistrate offers her the choice, not to return to the oasis with him but to go back to her people.

The equation between sex and torture is made explicit here and there further on in the novel, for example when the Magistrate imagines the barbarian girl saying to him in the midst of his failed attempts at lovemaking: "'That is not how you do it,' she should have said, stopping me in the act. 'If you want to learn how to do it, ask your friend with the black eyes [that is, Colonel Joll, her torturer, who wears dark glasses habitually].' Then she should have continued, so as not to leave me without hope. 'But if you want to love me you will have to turn your back on him and learn your lesson elsewhere.' If she had told me then, if I had understood her, if I had been in a position to understand her, if I had believed her, if I had been in a position to believe her, I might have saved myself from a year of confused and futile gestures of expiation" (WB, 156).

The cascade of "ifs" suggests how unlikely it is that we will learn in time or learn at all, or that any means of expiation exists: "To the last we will have learned nothing. In all of us, deep down, there seems to be something granite and unteachable" (WB, 165). That is a hard wisdom to accept. It suggests that the meaning and the art of meaning in *Waiting for the Barbarians* are incompatible. The former urges the reader to refer the story back to present history and to act constructively on that "self-disclosure" of the elements that have gone into the fictionalizing act. In their transgressed or transmogrified form those elements constitute a powerful indictment of the ideology of Empire, as well as of some ideologies of what is meant by sexually "possessing" the other. The art of meaning Coetzee employs suggests, on the contrary, that we can learn nothing and be led to do nothing effective either from life or from fictions as embodiments of the imaginary. Deep down, in all of us, there seems to be something granite and unteachable. That is what I mean by saying I find *Waiting for the Barbarians* deeply troubling to read, not exactly a benign expansion of my plasticity. The novel, or at least what the Magistrate says, teaches us that we are unteachable. Behind the Magistrate, however, there is, it may be, the effaced presence of Coetzee himself. Coetzee perhaps guards an unspoken ironic distance from the Magistrate. Coetzee perhaps may not, or perhaps may, wholly agree with the Magistrate's dark wisdom. As with ironic discourse in general, it is up to you to decide, though you will be unable to base your decision on sound evidence on either side.

Notes

1. Available in *Aspects of Narrative* (Selected Papers from the English Institute), ed. J. Hillis Miller (New York: Columbia University Press, 1971), and in Wolfgang Iser, *Prospecting: From Reader Response to Literary Anthropology* (Baltimore: The Johns Hopkins University Press, 1989), 3-30.

2. Wolfgang Iser, *The Fictive and the Imaginary: Charting Literary Anthropology* (Baltimore: The Johns Hopkins University Press, 1993), henceforth FIe; ibid., *Das Fiktive und das Imaginäre: Perspektiven literarische Anthropologie* (Frankfurt am Main: Suhrkamp, 1991), henceforth FIg. "Charting literary anthropology," by the way, is not a literal translation of the German subtitle, which means "perspectives on literary anthropology."

3. I am extremely grateful for the wise comments and questions from the audience after my presentation of this lecture at the University of Konstanz. Those comments have led to revisions here and there that have improved my lecture. See especially endnote 11 below.

4. Paul de Man, "'Conclusions': Walter Benjamin's 'The Task of the Translator,'" in *The Resistance to Theory* (Minneapolis: University of Minnesota Press, 1986), 88.

5. J.M. Coetzee, *Waiting for the Barbarians* (New York: Penguin, 2010), first published in 1980. Citations identified by WB followed by the page numbers.

6. "'A Child is being Beaten': A Contribution to the Study of the Origin of Sexual Perversions," in *The Standard Edition of the Complete Psychological Works of Sigmund Freud*, trans. James Strachey et al. (London: Vintage, Hogarth Press, and Institute of Psycho-Analysis, 2001), 17: 177-204.

7. Authoritative English translations of these and other stories by Kafka can be found in *Kafka's Selected Stories*, trans. and ed. Stanley Corngold, Norton Critical Edition (New York: W. W. Norton & Company, 2007).

8. Available bilingually in Franz Kafka, *Parables and Paradoxes* (New York: Schocken, 1961), 12-15.

9. Ha Jin, *Waiting* (New York: Vintage, 2000).

10. I have used this term as the title of an essay in *Derrida Today* (vol. 3 [May 2010], 75-91), to name a way of reading Wallace Stevens's "The Man on the Dump" as anticipatory of our present situation. Today climate change and human prodigality are turning the whole world into a garbage dump such as Stevens's poem describes. "Anachronistic reading" could also describe the reader's experience of the way Kafka's novels foreshadow the Holocaust. See my "Franz Kafka: Premonitions of Auschwitz," in *The Conflagration of Community: Fiction before and after Auschwitz* (Chicago: The University of Chicago Press, 2011), 39-145. Russell Samolsky in a brilliant new book, *Apocalyptic Futures: Marked Bodies and the Violence of the Text in Kafka, Conrad, and Coetzee* (New York: Fordham University Press, 2011) sets Kafka's "In the Penal Colony" and Coetzee's *Waiting for the Barbarians* side by side as parallel prefigurings of recent events in Abu Graib and Guantánamo Bay.

11. Monika Reif-Hülser, in extremely helpful comments on my lecture after its presentation in Konstanz, reminded me that this somewhat odd repeated episode of the Magistrate's washing and then rubbing with almond oil the barbarian girl's wounded body, especially her feet and ankles, echoes Mary Magdalene's touching anointing of Christ's feet in John 12: 3: "Then took Mary a pound of ointment of spikenard, very costly, and anointed the feet of Jesus, and wiped his feet with her hair: and the house was filled with the odor of the ointment." See also Matt. 26: 7 and Mark 14: 3, where Mary Magdalene pours the oil on Jesus's head, not his feet. The genders, you will notice, are reversed in Coetzee's version. I add yet another echo. In the marvelous Book Six of Homer's *The Odyssey*, "Nausicaa," first Nausicaa and her waiting maids and then Odysseus himself anoint themselves with olive oil from a golden flask after bathing. All three of these scenes are powerfully erotic.

III

A Defense Of Literature And Literary Study In A Time Of Globalization And The New Tele-Technologies

Marx and Engels, in a famous and quite remarkable paragraph in Chapter One of the *Communist Manifesto*, foresaw what today we call globalization, both as economic *mondialisation*, to give it its French name, and as cultural "world-wide-ification." I am thinking of the section in the *Manifesto* that begins with the claim that:

> All fixed, fast-frozen relations, with their train of ancient and venerable prejudices and opinions, are swept away, all new-formed ones become antiquated before they can ossify. All that is solid melts into air, all that is holy is profaned, and man is at last compelled to face with sober senses his real conditions of life, and his relations with his kind.
>
> The need of a constantly expanding market for its products chases the bourgeoisie over the entire surface of the globe. It must nestle everywhere, settle everywhere, establish connections everywhere.
>
> The bourgeoisie has through its exploitation of the world market given a cosmopolitan character to production and consumption in every country. To the great chagrin of Reactionists, it has drawn from under the feet of industry the national ground on which it stood. All old-established national industries have been destroyed or are daily being destroyed. They are dislodged by new industries, whose introduction becomes a life and death question for all civilized nations, by industries that no longer work up indigenous raw material, but raw material drawn from the remotest zones;

industries whose products are consumed, not only at home, but in every quarter of the globe.¹

This paragraph of the *Manifesto* ends with these prophetic sentences: "In place of old local and national seclusion and self-sufficiency, we have intercourse in every direction, universal inter-dependence of nations. And as in material, so also in intellectual production. The intellectual creations of individual nations become common property. National one-sidedness and narrow-mindedness become more and more impossible, and from numerous national and local literatures there arises a world literature" (ibid.). "World literature," *Weltliteratur* – the word and the idea are Goethe's. Though Marx did not foresee the iPod, he did understand what changes technological innovation make. Today he would be speaking not of world literature, but of an apparently homogenous worldwide culture of the new media: television, films, popular music, the internet, email, podcasts, videos, computer games, digital photos sent by email, and so on.

I have elsewhere emphasized that present-day globalization has three fundamental features: 1) Globalization is happening at different rates and in different ways in different countries and regions. 2) Globalization is heterogeneous, not one single happening. Several quite different forms of globalization are going on at the same time. Economic globalization is not the same thing as cultural globalization. Neither of these is the same thing as the globalization of technology, nor is the environmental degradation that is causing what is called "global warming" quite the same as any of these. 3) The common denominator of all these forms of globalization is new tele-techno-communication. Though Marx and Engels understood the way technology was already in 1848 changing the world and making globalization inevitable, they did not, of course, foresee radio, television, the cell phone, nor even the telephone and the gramophone. It is these forms of technology, the ones that make possible many new forms of communication at a distance, that have made globalization hyperbolic in scope and rapidity.

Marx and Engels saw the globalization of capitalism as both a catastrophe and an opportunity. It would be a catastrophe for the old European nation states because it would weaken their hegemonies. That weakening Marx and Engels more or less welcomed. Globalization would also mean, they foresaw, the victory of capitalism as a world-wide single economic system of exploitation, commodification, and commodity fetishism. That they deplored. They also saw global capitalism, however, as the chance for communism, through the death of capitalism when it inevitably over-reaches itself through a process of autoimmune self-destruction. The workers will rebel to usher in the dictatorship of the proletariat. Marx and Engels, you will remember, do not appeal to the workers of this or that nation to organize within that country and resist. They say, "Working men [sic!] of all countries, unite!" If Marx and Engels prophesied the globalization of capitalism, communism, as defined in the Manifesto, was itself explicitly a form of globalization. In this it was like Christianity, from which our conception of "the world" as a unified totality is derived. Marx and Engels also saw that both forms of globalization, economic and cultural, involve the weakening of nation state hegemonies and of national cultures, for better or for worse.

What possible role can there be for literary study in a time of cinema, television, the internet, podcasts, globally distributed popular music, computer games, and blogs? Literature would seem to be already a thing of the past, as Hegel said art was. Literary study would therefore seem to be no more than a species of antiquarianism. Or rather, it might be better to say that literature has moved from being the primary medium of virtual realities to being just one among many available purveyors of the imaginary, the spectral, the ghostly, the magical, the illusory. Literature now takes its place alongside cinema, television, the Internet, computer games, popular music, and iPods as another form of teletechnocommunications. Jacques Derrida calls them "artefactualities."[2]

What do I mean by saying that literature is a medium, like the new media, for the communication of virtual realities? I mean that when I read a printed novel or a poem the words on the page provide me access, if I am an adept reader, to a realm of people in a setting and in their interaction that seems like the "real world," that is, like the material world around me that I can see, smell, and touch, but that is available only, and exclusively, by way of those words on the page. In a similar way, television news looks like it is giving me direct access to events more or less as they are happening, but television images are elaborately filtered and reshaped, "cut and pasted" to produce a constituted pseudo-reality, a technologically manufactured realm of spooks and shadows that dance on the television screen. That, I suppose, is what Derrida means by calling television a purveyor of artefactualities. The images provided not only by the new media, but also by old ones like literature are apparent facts that are in fact artifacts. A computer game is quite obviously a virtual reality. Even a popular song has an implicit story. The song generates the sense of an imaginary situation in which someone might say or sing what the words of the song say or sing.

Why have these new media, in a way parallel to the success of the print novel when it first appeared in the late seventeenth century in Europe, had such an immediate appeal? Why did a million and a half Chinese pay good money to subscribe to the Chinese version of the computer game, *World of Warcraft*, when it came out in the summer of 2005? Now over three million Chinese play *World of Warcraft*.[3] Why this instant success? I answer that human beings seem to need virtual realities. We take insatiable pleasure in artefactualities. Human beings need fictions. They take to them as a duck takes to water, in whatever form they are most readily available. These new media purvey virtual realities in ways that are relatively easy to translate, transfer, or adapt all over the world, whereas printed literature is more tied to one natural language, to local idioms, and to local cultural conventions. A popular song can be successful, "popular," even in countries where the language is not understood. My formula, the knowing reader will note, significantly alters Aristotle's formulation in the *Poetics*. Aristotle said human beings take pleasure in imitation, *mimesis*, because they learn from imitations. The referential basis of imitation is retained by Aristotle and is essential for him. I say, on the contrary, that human beings need fictions that are not directly mimetic of anything. Such artefactualities create a new world presupposing the momentary displacement, forgetting, or even abolition of the "real world."

Two more things have happened to literature as a result of globalizing technologies, in addition to its relegation to the status of being just one among many ways to enter virtual realities. One is the globalization of literature, as Marx foresaw. Any national literature anywhere in the world, both those in "dominant" countries and those in "subordinate" countries (though that distinction is breaking down), exist now for many or most readers in the context or all the other literatures in all the other languages.

This happens partly through the extreme rapidity and diffusion of translations these days, partly through the global diffusion of certain languages, most obviously English. "Literature in English" is one form globalization is taking. British literature, like American literature, is just one segment of world literature in English. It seems increasingly foolish to study either British or American literature in isolation.

The second change in literature as a result of globalizing technologies is the radical transformation of literature study. As I have said in another paper, globalization of the new teletechnologies has meant the transformation of literary scholarship and the weakening of the necessity to do it in a university setting. Anyone anywhere now with a computer can have access to an enormous distributed database of scholarly information and online texts. These allow authoritative research in almost anything. It is becoming less and less necessary to own or to have access to that traditional basis of research and teaching in the humanities: lots of printed books, a "research library." It is not necessary, for example, to own hard copies, as they are called, of Henry James's novels. They are almost all available online for free. I have cited in this paper the *Communist Manifesto* from one among several online versions I obtained in a few seconds by way of *Google*. Collaborative scholarship can be carried on by teams that are made up of individuals spread all over the world, not just located in a single university. I was in 2005–2006 involved in an ambitious international research project on narratology. It was ostensibly located at the Center for Advanced Study in Oslo, though I spent a total of only three weeks there during the year. Research essays are written on a computer and sent anywhere in the world instantaneously as email attachments. I write all my letters of recommendation in the computer and send many of them by email. Dissertation chapters are sent to me by email. I am learning to read, annotate, and comment on them on the computer screen. The whole minute to minute process of my professional life as a student of literature has been utterly changed by the computer in a few short years.

Though I have found it difficult to put my finger on how literature in the sense of printed poems and novels is changed by being put within the context of globalizing teletechnocommunications, more and more absorbed within it, "digitized," as we say, like everything else, my strong feeling is that the change is fundamental. One important change is the ability to search so easily online versions of literary works. Another is the subjective sense the reader of online versions has that the work now exists in cyberspace, not in multiple copies of a book on library shelves. The digitizing of literature is the preparation for literature's disappearance in the form we have known it in the brief period of the printed book's dominance as the chief cultural medium. This period began in the late seventeenth-century in the West, the time of the rise of modern democracies, more or less universal literacy, and the more or less complete freedom to write or say whatever you like, never completely achieved anywhere, of course.

All honor to those scholars who have turned to so-called "cultural studies" and to studies of the new media. Those new media are enormously influential all over the world these days. It is natural that academics should want to study them, their contexts, and their influences. I want now, in conclusion, however, to defend literature and literary study in the fast-disappearing old-fashioned sense of printed books. I want to praise literary study in a time of globalization and new digitized media, often media that center on visual images rather than on written words. I want also to express my allegiance to so-called "modernist" literature in Europe and America. That segment of literature has especially, among other things, brought the essence of literature, what it is and what it can do, out into the open or at least into shadowy semi-visibility. I want, finally, to "come clean" and to admit that I believe literature can say things and do things that cannot be done, or that are almost impossible to do, in the newer media. Those things go against these new media's grain. They are nevertheless of great value, perhaps even indispensable, irreplaceable, value, even though we may well soon have dispensed with literature without the world or human civilization coming to an end.

Just what are those things that only printed literature can do or do best? A comparison between canonical novels and even the best films made from these novels, such as recent British films or television productions of novels by Jane Austen, Charles Dickens, George Eliot, Anthony Trollope, Thomas Hardy, Henry James, and E. M. Forster, will give one answer. As carefully as these films follow the novels, as brilliant as they often are as cinema, they find it virtually impossible to carry over into the new medium one essential feature of printed novels. I mean the ironic doubling of the character's language by the narrator's language in what is called "free indirect discourse." As numerous scholars have shown, free indirect discourse, narrative language that repeats the character's putative present tense internal language in the third person past tense, is fundamentally undecidable. It is impossible to tell for sure whether we are reading the character's own language or the narrator's language. Two things follow from this: 1) A gift for irony is a necessity for good reading of printed literature in a way that is not the case, or not so much the case, for playing computer games, appreciating a popular song, or watching a film. 2) Printed literature, even the simplest and most straightforward of written fictive sentences, hides a secret.[4] As Derrida puts this in *Passions*, speaking of his passion for literature, *il y a là du secret*, there is there some secret. Literature's secret can never be revealed or brought into the open. It remains hidden behind the appearances that tell of it. This secret is not a matter of the greater verbal or figural complexity that is often mistakenly thought to be a distinctive characteristic of literary language. Such complexity is a feature of written language generally, for example in the puns in newspaper headlines: "Airline Profits Head for Nosedive."

The secret that there is there in literature is revealed and hidden in the simplest literary sentence. Franz Kafka said he became a writer when he substituted *er* for *ich*, he for I. The early parts of one of his masterpieces, *Das Schloß*, [*The Castle*], were first written in the first person and then rewritten in the third person, thereby enigmatically doubling the represented consciousness in the way I have said free indirect discourse does. In a remarkable statement, Kafka said, "When I write without calculation a sentence like the following: 'He looked out the window,' this sentence is already perfect."[5] By "perfect," as the context makes clear, Kafka meant that the full perfection of all literature can do is already present in such a sentence, since it creates magically a virtual or fictive world. The initial paragraph of Kafka's first great story, "Das Urteil," "The Judgment," the story that confirmed for him his gifts as a writer, culminates in such a sentence: "Er ... sah dann, den Ellbogen auf den Schreibtisch gestützt, aus dem fenster auf den Fluß, die Brücke und die Anhöhen am anderen Ufer mit ihrem schwachen Grün."[6] (He looked then, his elbows planted on the table, out the window toward the river, the bridge, and the high ground on the other shore with its tender green. [my translation]). A diary entry describes the writing of this story, which took place all during one night, as both the total destruction by fire of the "real world," and the simultaneous creation, in a Phoenix-like resurrection brought about performatively by the words he set down or inscribed one by one on the page, of a unique, alternative literary world, a virtual reality. Kafka also defines the act of writing as lifting oneself by one's bootstraps, as the saying goes. Writing is an impossible carrying oneself on one's own back. He asserts also that "everything can be said," that is, that everything whatsoever can be turned into literature: "The fearful strain and joy, how the story developed before me, as if I were advancing over water. Several times during this night I heaved my own weight on my back. How everything can be said, how for everything, for the strangest fancies, there waits a great fire in which they perish and rise up again."[7]

A famous sentence in Mallarmé's "Crise de vers" ("Crisis of Verse") says something similar in a different, distinctively Mallarméan, idiom, this time in terms of poetic speaking rather than writing: "Je dis: une fleur! et, hors de l'oubli où ma voix relègue aucun contour, en tant que quelque chose d'autre que les calices sus, musicalement se lève, idée même et suave, l'absente de tous bouquets."[8] (I say, a flower! and, outside the forgetting to which my voice relegates every contour, as something other than the known calyxes, musically there rises, suave idea itself, the something absent from all bouquets. [my translation]) Mallarmé's formulation is embedded in the local idiom of his time and place. Mallarmé was fond of fancy words, especially words in "x," such as "calyx" or, in French, "calice," from Latin "calyx," which means "the outer protective covering of a flower." "Musically" has as its context the primacy of rhythm in Mallarmé's poetics and the fin de siècle notion that all the arts aspire to the condition of music. Mallarmé's word "idea" has Hegelian resonances, as in Hegel's definition of the beautiful, in the *Lectures on Aesthetics*, as "das sinnliche Scheinen der Idee," the sensible shining forth, or appearance, of the idea. That figure of shining reappears in the poem by Wallace Stevens I discuss below. Nevertheless, in spite of these singularities, Mallarmé is saying something similar to what Kafka said. The simplest language, "He looked out of the window," or "a flower," is the abolition not only of the object it names, but also of the whole material world to which it appears to refer, and of which windows and flowers are familiar parts. At the same time, such language is the performative creation of a fictive world that reveals and hides what Jacques Derrida calls "le tout autre,"[9] the wholly other, named by Mallarmé here as "idea," a word crucial for Wallace Stevens too, as when, in "Notes Toward a Supreme Fiction," he exhorts the "ephebe," or novice, to "see the sun again with an ignorant eye/And see it clearly in the idea of it."[10]

I conclude by demonstrating, in a sketch or hypotyposis, how the simplicity of literary language indicates, without revealing, a secret, something wholly other. My example is the next to the last poem in Wallace Stevens' *Collected Poems*. It is a poem written in the poet's old age, when he lived in the shadow of death. Death is named in the poem by way of references to the River Styx of Greek mythology. Stevens calls the realm of the dead "Stygia." The poem is called "The River of Rivers in Connecticut." This poem is rooted in local idiom, in local culture, and in local topography near the city of Hartford, where Stevens lived. The name "Connecticut," according to Wikipedia, "comes from the Mohegan Indian word 'Quinnehtukqut' meaning 'Long River Place' or 'Beside the Long Tidal River.'" Stevens' title appears, at least at first, to refer to the Connecticut River, one of America's great rivers. That river bisects the state of Connecticut, a small New England state on the eastern coast of the United States. The poem names two towns near the Connecticut River, Farmington and Haddam. Both towns have beautiful late eighteenth or early nineteenth-century white-painted clapboard homes, churches, and civic buildings, in a serenely decorous and harmonious style called "Greek Revival." That style is one of the great triumphs of American architecture.

A careful reading of the poem indicates, however, that the river of rivers in Connecticut names not the Connecticut River, but an invisible ubiquitous river, neither transcendent nor immanent, definitely *not* an idealist transcendental, not an "idea" in the Platonic sense, but a river that "flows nowhere, like the sea." The river of rivers in Connecticut is "a curriculum, a vigor, a *local* abstraction." It flows ("curriculum") and it has power ("vigor"), but it is as much local as Haddam or Farmington. This "river" is Stevens's version of Mallarmé's "idée"; Kafka's "Gesetz," law, as in his parable, "Vor dem Gesetz," "Before the Law," in *Der Prozeß*,

The Trial; or Derrida's "tout autre," wholly other; or Derrida's untellable secret, "if there is one," as he says. It would be a mistake to think of this "wholly other" as one single monolithic or even monotheistic transcendent nameless "something." If "every other is wholly other," then each encounter-without-encounter of it is singular, unique, a local abstraction. Every wholly other is, by definition, wholly different from every other wholly other, as well as wholly different from me. The wholly other must be thought of as a swarming plurality, not a oneness, an *Einheit*. As Derrida says in the last sentence of "Psyché: Invention de l'autre," "L'autre appelle à venir et cela n'arrive qu'à plusieurs voix."[11]

I have said Stevens's title "names" this strange river. The word "names" is important, since it indicates that what the poem talks about is not really a river. The poet only *calls* it a river, in a performative catachresis that gives a name to the nameless secret that the scenery of the poem everywhere tells of without making visible. The poem depends on distinctions between seeing, naming, and telling. The river of rivers in Connecticut is "not to be seen beneath the appearances that *tell* of it" (my italics). The poet, in his answer or response to this telling, that is, in his poem, cannot directly name or refer to this river, since it is incompatible with referential language. It is an "unnamed flowing." The poet can only *call* it something that is not literally what it is. The poet can only, "call it, again and again,/ The river that flows nowhere, like a sea." This calling is more a performative invocation than a referential naming, even a catachrestic one.

Here is a link to the poem: http://www.poemhunter.com/poem/the-river-of-rivers-in-connecticut/

"The river of rivers" is not really the name of this secret "something" in Connecticut. That is just what the poet calls it. It is actually an "unnamed flowing," but even "flowing" is a word borrowed from the name for what real rivers do. No language can name this river of rivers, except by indirection, though "indirection" is not an adequate word for this performative response to the unnamable.

This beautiful and moving poem calls forth endless commentary, for example the provocative phrase about "trees that lack the intelligence of trees." This wonderful phrase does not mean that trees are smart. It rather transfers our knowledge of trees, this side of Stygia, to the trees themselves. When we get to those black cataracts of Stygia, the realm of death, we shall forget all human knowledge. The river Stevens calls out to, however, is "far this side of Stygia." This is a poem about life under the sunlight in Connecticut, not about the realm of death. No shadow walks beside this river, such as the shadows that walk on Stygia's banks. Stevens's river is not black with death and lack of intelligence. Its "mere flowing," rather, is full of "a gayety,/flashing and flashing in the sun." Something could be said at length about every word and phrase in this poem, for example about the admirable lines that show a revelation-without-revelation through shining and glistening, even though the river of rivers is not to be seen beneath the appearances that tell of it: "The steeple at Farmington/ Stands glistening, and Haddam shines and sways."

As Jacques Derrida has abundantly shown, for example, this connection without connection of literature with the wholly other has crucial implications for the ethical and political functioning of literature.[12] Can the newer magical media—film, television, computer games, popular music, and so on, do anything with words or other signs comparable to what Stevens so effortlessly does with the printed word? Perhaps, but with great difficulty, and in ways that are hardly noticeable, or at any rate that are not noticed by most of the scholars who write about the new media. For most of them, "other" means the racial, national, linguistic, ethnic, or gender other, not Derrida's "tout autre." It sounds absurd to claim that the computer game *World of Warcraft* keeps a secret, in the sense that Derrida means "secret," though it might be worth trying to demonstrate that this is the case. I conclude therefore that what we call written literature has an almost unique and irreplaceable performative function in human culture, even in a time of globalization and the increasing dominance of new teletechnologicoprestidigitizing media.

Notes

1. http://www.marxists.org/archive/marx/works/1848/communist-manifesto/ch01.htm
2. Here is one among many places where Derrida uses this neologism: Jacques Derrida, *On Touching-Jean-Luc Nancy*, trans. Christine Irizarry (Stanford: Stanford University Press, 2005), 301.

3. See the story in *The New York Times* for Sept. 5, 2006: http://www.nytimes.com/2006/ 09/05/technology/05wow. Of the global success of World of Warcraft (WOW), one can only say, "Wow!"

4. Jacques Derrida, *Passions* (Paris: Galilée, 1993), 56–71.

5. Cited in Maurice Blanchot, "Kafka et la littérature," *De Kafka à Kafka* (Paris: Gallimard, 1981), 81, my translation.

6. Franz Kafka, *Die Verwandlung und Andere Erzählungen* (Köln: Könemann, 1955), 35.

7. Franz Kafka, *The Diaries: 1910–1922*, ed. Max Brod, trans. Joseph Kresh and Martin Greenberg, with the cooperation of Hannah Arendt (New York: Schocken, n.d.), 212–213.

8. Stéphane Mallarmé, "Crise de vers," *Oeuvres complètes*, ed. Henri Mondor and G. Jean-Aubry, ed. de la Pléiade (Paris: Gallimard, 1945), 368.

9. Jacques Derrida, *Donner la mort* (Paris: Galilée, 1999), 114–117.

10. ll. 5–6 of "It Must Be Abstract," the first section of "Notes Toward a Supreme Fiction," in Wallace Stevens, *The Collected Poems* (New York: Vintage, 1990), 380.

11. The other calls to come [or, calls the future] and that does not happen [or arrive] except in multiple voices [my translation].

12. See, for example, "La littérature au secret: Une filiation impossible," the second essay in the French version of *Donner la mort*, 159–209. This important essay has been translated into English by Adam Kotsko and circulated here and there by email, but has not, so far as I know, yet been published in printed form.

IV

Ecotechnics
Ecotechnological Odradek

Humanity [must] ... furnish the effort necessary in order to get accomplished ... the essential function of the universe, which is a machine for making gods.

Henri Bergson

Our world is the world of the "technical," a world whose cosmos, nature, gods, entire system, is, in its inner joints, exposed as "technical": the world of an ecotechnical. The ecotechnical functions with technical apparatuses, to which our every part is connected. But what it makes are our bodies, which it brings into the world and links to the system, thereby creating our bodies as more visible, more proliferating, more polymorphic, more compressed, more "amassed" and "zoned" than ever before. Through the creation of bodies the ecotechnical has the sense that we vainly seek in the remains of the sky or the spirit.

Jean-Luc Nancy, Corpus

[The universe] knits us in and it knits us out. It has knitted time space, pain, death, corruption, despair, and all the illusions—and nothing matters.

Joseph Conrad, Letters to Cunninghame Graham

Technology as Model

"Eco" comes from the Greek word *oikos*, the house or home. The prefix "eco-" is used more broadly now to refer to the total environment within which one or another "living" creature "dwells." Each creature dwells in its "ecosystem." Included in that system are other circumambient creatures—viruses, bacteria, plants, and animals—but also the climate in the broad sense of the environment. The ecosystem also includes "technical apparatuses." I mean all those manmade teletechnological devices like television sets, iPhones, and computers connected to the Internet, into which our bodies are plugged.

I would add this to Nancy's formulation: The total environment more and more reveals itself to be "technological," that is, in one way or another machinelike. The "body" is, according to Nancy "linked" to its technological ecosystem in manifold ways, as a prosthesis of a prosthesis. That body, however, is more and more being shown also to function like a machine. It is a technical product of the ecotechnical. "The body" is a complex set of interlocking mechanisms that are self-generating, self-regulating, and self-reading sign systems. "There is no 'the' body," (*"il n'y a pas 'le' corps"*), in the sense of a unitary organism, says Jean-Luc Nancy (*Corpus* 104). These corporeal sign systems are the products of chance permutations extending over millions of years, such as those that have produced the human genome. These sign systems do not depend on human consciousnesses or on actions based on the choice of a voluntary code-reader in order to function. They just go on working and unworking.

This essay focuses on Kafka's uncanny little story, if it can be called a story, "*Die Sorge des Hausvaters*" ("The Worry of the Father of the Family") (1919). I use Kafka's 474 word text as a way of thinking what results from a shift from an organic unity model to a technological model as a paradigm for thinking in various domains. My essay might be called a thought experiment. "What would happen if . . . we used a technological model rather than an organic model to understand X?" Whether Kafka's text can be "used" as a way of thinking about this or about anything else, or whether anything at all can be done with "*Die Sorge des Hausvaters*," remains to be seen. It does not go without saying.

Among the domains to be subjected to my thought experiment are languages, human and inhuman; sign systems generally; literature and literary criticism, along with literary theory; "life," "the body," the immune system, the endocrine system, the brain, consciousness, the unconscious, the self or "ego"; the atom-molecule-thing-virus-bacterium-vegetable-animal-human being sequence; societies, both human and inhuman, communities, nations, and cultures; history; the Internet and other such teletechnological assemblages (radio, telephone, television, cell-phones, iPhones, etc.); the global financial system; the environment, the weather, climate change; astrophysics from the Big Bang to whatever endless end the cosmos may reach. According to many scientists, the universe's expansion is apparently accelerating. Galaxies are gradually getting so far apart that ultimately no light or other signals will be able to get from one to any other. Talk about the Pascalian "silence of infinite spaces"! The iPhone will be of no use then.

The organic unity model has had a tenacious hold on thinking in the West from the Greeks and the Bible down to Heidegger and present-day eco-poets and extollers of "the body." We tend, moreover, to think of organisms as "animated" in one way or another. An organism is inhabited and held together by a soul (*anima*) or by some principle of life. Consciousness, mind, the ego, the soul animate human bodies, just as animals, trees, flowers, and the earth as a whole are alive, animated by an integrated principle of life, and just as dead letters, the materiality of language, the marks on the page, are animated by a meaning inherent in a collection of letters and spaces. As Martin Heidegger, notoriously, expresses this, "*Die Sprache spricht.*" Language speaks (210), as though it were animated by an *anima*. Another way to put this is to say that anthropomorphisms and prosopopoeias have been ubiquitous in our tradition as grounds for formulations in many domains. John Ruskin called these personifications "pathetic fallacies." The Book of Numbers in the Old Testament, for example, asserts that "If the Lord make a new thing, and the earth open her mouth, and swallow them up, with all that appertain unto them, and they go down quick into the pit; then ye shall understand that these men have provoked the Lord" (Num. 16:30). Isaiah, in a passage cited by Ruskin, asserts that "the mountains and the hills shall break forth before you into singing, and all the trees of the field shall clap their hands" (Isa. 55:12). Ruskin calls this a justifiable pathetic fallacy because it deals with God's power, that is, with something that is infinitely beyond human understanding and language. St. Paul speaks of the way "the whole creation groaneth and travaileth in pain" (Rom. 8:22), as though the creation were an animate creature. A living thing, whether vegetable, animal, or human, is to be distinguished from dead matter by its organic unity. Every part works with the others to make that living thing more than a mechanical assemblage of parts. The human ego or self we think of as organically unified. We tend to think of a "natural language" as an organic unity of words organized by an innate, universal, grammar and syntax, such as that imagined by Noam Chomsky. A good community is an organically unified set of assumptions and behaviors. History is made of transitions from one set of such assumptions and behaviors to the next, in a series of Foucauldian "epistemes," with inexplicable leaps between. Some of today's eco-poets, like many native peoples, imagine the earth as a quasi-personified "Pan-Gaia," Mother Earth. This lovely lady has human beings under her benevolent care, so we need not fear that climate change will harm us. Mama Earth would not let that happen. The "organic unity" model of a good poem or other literary work has had great force from the Romantics to the New Critics. If it is a good poem, it must be organically unified, with all its parts working harmoniously together to make a beautiful object like a flower or like the body of a graceful woman.

Martin Heidegger, in *The Fundamental Concepts of Metaphysics: World, Solitude, Finitude,* asserts that the stone is world-less, *weltlos,* the animal is poor in world, *weltarm,* whereas human beings are world-building, *weltbilden* (389-416; original 268-87). A "world" is implicitly a whole, once more an organic unity. We tend to assume that in one way or another technology names a human process of making out of parts assembled together something that is in some way useful, a prosthetic tool extending man's power and a product of his ingenuity, inventiveness, and manufacturing power. A technological artifact is not animated, though we tend to personify our machines, to refer to our automobiles, for example, as "she." *Techné* is opposed to *Physis,* just as subject is opposed to object. *Techné* is a skill manipulated by subjectivities and their bodies. Technology adds something to a nature thought of as already externally out there and as organic. Heidegger hated modern technological gadgets. He refused to use a typewriter. Only a man holding a pen can think, he thought, that is, do "what is called thinking." Human beings think with their pens. Heidegger saw the wholesale technologizing of Russia and the United States, and, through them, the technologizing of the whole world, as rapidly bringing true organic civilization, that is Greek and German culture, to an end.[1] "Only a God will save us," he said on the famous occasion of an interview with *Der Spiegel*. He would no doubt have found the present global triumph of teletechnology abominable. We tend, however, even to personify our computers and the Internet. We feel that there is a God in the machine. Our prosthetic gadgets think and work for themselves, not always along the lines we want them to work and think.

Such examples of the organic unity model could be multiplied indefinitely. They are everywhere. Who would dare to say of them what Ruskin says of one of his examples of the pathetic fallacy ("The spendthrift crocus, bursting through the mould/Naked and shivering, with his cup of gold"): "This is very beautiful, and yet very untrue" (par. 4).

The alternative techno-machinal model has also a long history going back at least to Leibniz, to the idea of a watchmaker God, to such eighteenth-century books as de la Mettrie's *L'homme machine*, and down to recent work that thinks of the human immune system as more machine-like than organic, or to the rejection of anthropomorphisms in thinking of the cosmos or of climate change. Our presupposed paradigm of the machine, however, has mutated over the last century from examples like the steam engine and the internal combustion engine to forms of technology that are embodied sign-systems or communications machines, like television, iPhones, and a computer connected to the Internet. Even automobiles these days are computerized. They are as much complex sign systems as they are gas-powered engines to turn the car's wheels. Before looking a little more closely at the strange features of the ecotechnological model, however, I turn to Kafka as an exemplary thinker/non-thinker of the inhumanly machinal.

Machinal Auto-Co-Immunity as Context: Our Present State of Emergency

I do so, however, in a context. I am thinking not of the context of the important discussions between Walter Benjamin and Gershom Scholem, is, do "what is called thinking." Human beings think with their pens. Heidegger saw the wholesale technologizing of Russia and the United States, and, through them, the technologizing of the whole world, as rapidly bringing true organic civilization, that is Greek and German culture, to an end.[1] "Only a God will save us," he said on the famous occasion of an interview with *Der Spiegel*. He would no doubt have found the present global triumph of teletechnology abominable. We tend, however, even to personify our computers and the Internet. We feel that there is a God in the machine. Our prosthetic gadgets think and work for themselves, not always along the lines we want them to work and think.

Such examples of the organic unity model could be multiplied indefinitely. They are everywhere. Who would dare to say of them what Ruskin says of one of his examples of the pathetic fallacy ("The spendthrift crocus, bursting through the mould/Naked and shivering, with his cup of gold"): "This is very beautiful, and yet very untrue" (par. 4).

The alternative techno-machinal model has also a long history going back at least to Leibniz, to the idea of a watchmaker God, to such eighteenth-century books as de la Mettrie's *L'homme machine*, and down to recent work that thinks of the human immune system as more machine-like than organic, or to the rejection of anthropomorphisms in thinking of the cosmos or of climate change. Our presupposed paradigm of the machine, however, has mutated over the last century from examples like the steam engine and the internal combustion engine to forms of technology that are embodied sign-systems or communications machines, like television, iPhones, and a computer connected to the Internet. Even automobiles these days are computerized. They are as much complex sign systems as they are gas-powered engines to turn the car's wheels. Before looking a little more closely at the strange features of the ecotechnological model, however, I turn to Kafka as an exemplary thinker/non-thinker of the inhumanly machinal.

Machinal Auto-Co-Immunity as Context: Our Present State of Emergency

I do so, however, in a context. I am thinking not of the context of the important discussions between Walter Benjamin and Gershom Scholem, human understanding and language. St. Paul speaks of the way "the whole creation groaneth and travaileth in pain" (Rom. 8:22), as though the creation were an animate creature. A living thing, whether vegetable, animal, or human, is to be distinguished from dead matter by its organic unity. Every part works with the others to make that living thing more than a mechanical assemblage of parts. The human ego or self we think of as organically unified. We tend to think of a "natural language" as an organic unity of words organized by an innate, universal, grammar and syntax, such as that imagined by Noam Chomsky. A good community is an organically unified set of assumptions and behaviors. History is made of transitions from one set of such assumptions and behaviors to the next, in a series of Foucauldian "epistemes," with inexplicable leaps between. Some of today's eco-poets, like many native peoples, imagine the earth as a quasi-personified "Pan-Gaia," Mother Earth. This lovely lady has human beings under her benevolent care, so we need not fear that climate change will harm us. Mama Earth would not let that happen. The "organic unity" model of a good poem or other literary work has had great force from the Romantics to the New Critics. If it is a good poem, it must be organically unified, with all its parts working harmoniously together to make a beautiful object like a flower or like the body of a graceful woman.

Martin Heidegger, in *The Fundamental Concepts of Metaphysics: World, Solitude, Finitude,* asserts that the stone is world-less, *weltlos*, the animal is poor in world, *weltarm*, whereas human beings are world-building, *weltbilden* (389-416; original 268-87). A "world" is implicitly a whole, once more an organic unity. We tend to assume that in one way or another technology names a human process of making out of parts assembled together something that is in some way useful, a prosthetic tool extending man's power and a product of his ingenuity, inventiveness, and manufacturing power. A technological artifact is not animated, though we tend to personify our machines, to refer to our automobiles, for example, as "she." *Techné* is opposed to *Physis*, just as subject is opposed to object. *Techné* is a skill manipulated by subjectivities and their bodies. Technology adds something to a nature thought of as already externally out there and as organic. Heidegger hated modern technological gadgets. He refused to use a typewriter. Only a man holding a pen can think, he thought, that or between Benjamin and Berthold Brecht, on the question of whether Kafka is to be thought of as a mystic in the tradition of the Kabbalah or, on the contrary, as a faithful recorder of social conditions in pre-Holocaust Prague.[2] My context, rather, is our situation here in the United States and in the world today. Why and how should I read Kafka's *"Die Sorge des Hausvaters"* today, this moment, on November 4, 2011? It does not go without saying that reading this little text is at all useful and justifiable in our present state of emergency.

What is that emergency? The United States is engaged full-tilt in four radical forms of apparently unwitting "auto-co-immune" self-destruction, to borrow Jacques Derrida's neologism. The systems that should save and protect us are turning against ourselves.

One form of our suicidal folly is the refusal to move immediately to universal single-payer health care as the only way to keep health care costs from escalating further and further as a percentage of our GDP. That cost is already 16% of GDP, or even, according to some estimates, 20%, at least twice that of most European countries. This absurdity is bankrupting thousands when they get sick, killing tens of thousands of people every year who cannot afford health care, but also bankrupting the country, at the expense of making pharmaceutical companies and health insurance companies fathomlessly rich.

Another folly is the refusal to do anything serious to regulate the suicidal greed and risk-taking of banks and other financial institutions. Subprime mortgage-based credit default swaps and complex "derivatives" are the conspicuous example of this folly and greed. A minor consequence of the present "financial meltdown" is the dismantling of our educational system, especially public universities and especially the humanities. Our universities are in lock-step with finance capitalism. Harvard University lost about forty per cent of its endowment in the meltdown. Nothing has been done, for example raising taxes on the rich and large corporations, to ameliorate the outrageous discrepancy between the wealth of the top 1% and the remaining 99%. That 1% has survived the meltdown with increased income, wealth, and political power enabled through their manipulation of the media and "buying" of Congress.

A third form of auto-immune self-destruction is the refusal to withdraw from a disastrous war in Afghanistan, that "graveyard of empires."

Complete troop withdrawal is now scheduled for 2014. I hope I can be pardoned for being skeptical about whether that promise will be kept. It depends on who is in charge at that point. If Alexander the Great, the British, and the Soviet Union could not conquer and pacify that country, we are unlikely to be able to do it, even with a draft, millions of troops, and the further destruction of our economy, though of course the industrial buildup for WWII actually pulled our economy out of a decade of depression. It put everyone to work making guns, ammunition, tanks, and planes that would be then destroyed on the battlefield, in a triumph of the military-industrial complex.

The fourth looming catastrophe is the worst. It makes the others look trivial. We are doing practically nothing to keep this catastrophe from happening. Humanly caused global climate change, all but a tiny majority of scientists tell us, is most likely already irreversible. It is even now leading to more violent hurricanes, typhoons, and wild fires, the transformation of the United States Southwest into an arid desert, polar ice melt, tundra defrosting, glacial melting in Greenland, and so on. The ice and permafrost melting is generating feedback mechanisms that are raising global temperatures to lethal levels. The disastrous consequences of all these suicidal actions were more or less unintentional, though after a certain point we should have been able to see what was happening. The mystery is why we did nothing until it was too late. The internal combustion engine, chemical agriculture, and coal-fired electricity plants seemed like really neat ideas. They seemed to be technological inventions whose implementation would lead to improved quality of life all around. In a similar way, it seems a neat idea to be able to talk to or "text" to anyone anywhere in the world on a cell phone, though the concomitant changes in community and society were not at first evident. I mean the way these telecommunication gadgets are producing a mutation in the human species. The medium is the maker, and one thing it makes is the nature and collective culture of the human beings who use a given medium.[3] Global climate change on the scale it is happening will lead to widespread species extinction, water wars, the inundation of coastal plains worldwide (Florida, India, Vietnam, Australia, the Northeastern United States, where I live, small Pacific island nations, etc.), and perhaps ultimately to the extinction of *homo sapiens*, those wise creatures.

It is a feature of all four of these interlocked systems that changes in them are the product of chance, of random acts that statistically add up to a pattern. These systems are explicable by chaos and catastrophe theory. This means that they are all subject to sudden catastrophic change when they reach a certain unpredictable tipping point, as in the sudden unforeseen, but foreseeable, collapse of the investment companies Bear Stearns and Lehman Brothers, and the insurance giant AIG. Those collapses triggered the recent worldwide "financial meltdown." Another famous example is the way the flap of a butterfly's wing in Guatemala can, we are told, trigger a destructive hurricane in the Gulf of Mexico.

I can understand the head in the sand resistance to thinking about these linked domains and then trying to do something about them. Human beings have a limitless capacity for denial, for kidding themselves. *Homo sapiens*' possession of sapience, however, suggests that we should at least have a look around as the water rises above our chins. How can we explain, if not stop, our penchant for self-destruction? Part of the problem of course is that we are not objective witnesses. We are ourselves part of these self-destructive processes, one element in interlocking stochastic system we only think we can control. I claim Kafka's text might help us confront what is happening. That is a big and problematic claim.

Odradek the Illegible

What makes the reader queasy about *"Die Sorge des Hausvaters"*? This slight seasickness is brought about by the way this text resists being read according to any of the comforting organic unity models. These models are so ingrained as to be taken for granted. That is the case in general with ideological prejudices.

The English reader's problems begin with the title and with the question of its translation, not to speak of the translation of the text itself. Stanley Corngold's admirable new translation of Kafka's stories translates *"Die Sorge des Hausvaters"* as "The Worry of the Father of the Family." Peter Fenves, the translator of Werner Hamacher's essay, gives "Cares" for *"Sorge"*: "Cares of a Family Man" (118). It is not entirely easy for an English speaker to get the hang of the nuances of the word *"Sorge,"* as it is used in German. My German/English dictionary gives a whole set of not entirely compatible meanings for "*Sorge*": "grief, sorrow; worry, apprehension, anxiety, care, trouble, uneasiness, concern." This list is followed by a diverse set of idiomatic phrases employing "*Sorge*," e.g. "*die Sorge ertränken*" or "*ersäufen*," to drown one's sorrows in drink, and "*keine Sorge*," "Don't worry," "Never fear." That is somewhat like what we say today: "No problem."

Readers of Heidegger will remember the quite specific use he makes in *Sein und Zeit* of "Sorge," as distinguished from "*besorgen*," "*Besorgnis*," "*Fürsorge*," and "*versorgen*," not to speak of "*Angst*." Macquarrie and Robinson translate "*Sorge*" as "care." Chapter Six of Section One of *Sein und Zeit* is called "*Die Sorge als Sein des Daseins*" ("Care as the Being of *Dasein*"), and "*Sorge*" is firmly distinguished from "*Angst*," anxiety. Earlier Heidegger distinguished, in the permutations of words in "*Sorge*," between "*Besorgnis*," the "concern" we have for things ready to hand, from "*Fürsorge*," the "solicitude" we have for other *Daseins*, in our primordial condition of "being with" other *Daseins*. Each is a different form of "*Sorge*," care. (*Being and Time* 227, 157-9; original 182, 121-2). Is what the "*Hausvater*" suffers "care," or "concern," or "anxiety," or just "worry"? Just what is he worried about? What are his cares? The text is not entirely clear about that, but we shall see what we shall see.

"*Hausvater*" brings its own problems. No straightforward English equivalent exists, since "the father of the family" does not carry the implication of patriarchal domination and responsibility within the house. The Greek word "*oikonomos*" meant manager of a household, from "*oikos*," house, and "*nomos*," managing, or lawgiving. "*Hausvater*" is a precise enough translation of "*oikonomos*." "Eco" as in "economy," or "ecology," or "ecotechnology" refers to the house in the extended sense of "environment." An "ecosystem," says the *American Heritage Dictionary*, is "an ecological community together with its physical environment, considered as a unit." The whole earth can be thought of as one large ecosystem that is now undergoing rapid climate change, or change in the house within which all earthlings dwell together in a global village. Jean-Luc Nancy's term "ecotechnological" suggests that the whole environment is to be thought of under the aegis of the technological. This is a pantechnologization into which we and our bodies are plugged as a flash memory stick is plugged into a computer's USB connection, ready to receive whatever information is downloaded into it.

I have not even yet quite finished with the title. Who assigned the title? Who is to be imagined as speaking it? Presumably Franz Kafka, the author, who gave a name to what he had written. He had a right to do that, as a *Textvater*. Who then speaks the text? Presumably the *Hausvater*, who says of Odradek authoritatively informed things like, "Sometimes he disappears for months at a time; he has probably moved into other houses; but then he inevitably returns to our house (*doch kehrt er dann unweigerlich wieder in unser Haus zurück*)" (73). Since both title and text seem to be spoken or written in versions of Kafka's characteristically neutral, deadpan voice, it is hard to know how much irony the title directs at the concern, care, sorrow, or worry of the house-father. Is Odradek really anything the *Hausvater* ought to worry about? The house-father perhaps has more serious things at hand that ought to generate concern. "*Sorge*," however the reader takes it, seems, at least at first, an excessive term for what Odradek might justifiably cause.

If my reader thinks I am paying too much attention to nitpicking questions of translation and semantics, the first paragraph of "*Die Sorge des Hausvaters*" is my model and justification. It does not yet describe Odradek. Rather it speculates, fruitlessly, about the word's etymology and meaning. I agree it is a strange word, but are not all proper names strange, singular, unique? Nevertheless, they all tend to have semantic meaning, as does my family name, "Miller," or my wife's given name, "Dorothy": "gift of God."

Before looking at what the text says about the word "Odradek," let me, in the interest of getting on with what might become an interminable reading, suggest a working hypothesis. I claim that the name "Odradek," the "thing" called Odradek, the text about Odradek, and the implied speaker(s) of the title and text have a common destructuring technological structure. "Structure" is not an entirely good word for what I am trying to describe, since it suggests a static assemblage. The oxymoron "destructuring structure" suggests not only that the assemblage in question is in a process of constant dynamic movement, but also that this movement is in one way or another a dismantling, I would even dare to say a deconstructuring.

The relation among the four odd deconstructuring structures I have identified is difficult to name. The relation is not metaphorical, nor allegorical, nor even exactly analogical. Perhaps one might say these structures are in resonance, or consonance, or *Stimmung*. The resonance, however, is not exactly a harmonious chiming. It is more a *"Klang."* All are dissonant versions of one another.

The best model I know to describe these strange structures is to say that they are all are extremely peculiar little machines, each one *sui generis*, unlike all the others except in being strangely and contradictorily machinelike. What is machine-like about these structures, and what is peculiar about them if we think of them as machines? Each is made of parts that are assembled or articulated to make something that *works*. It does something, like any good machine. Each is both machine-like and also a self-functioning sign-system. Each seems in some way the product of *techné*, of an art of know-how. Each, however, is in one way or another incomplete or fissured, fractured by a crack, or cracks. Moreover, each forbids rational description or explanation. Each seems to be lacking meaning and identifiable purpose. The maker, finally, of these little unworked or inoperative (*désoeuvrées*[4]) machines cannot be easily identified, nor can one imagine what weird intention motivated his (her? its?) exercise of a manufacturing technique. Each of these non-machinal machines has what Walter Benjamin, speaking of Kafka's parables and stories, called a "cloudy place," a place where reasonable understanding and interpretation fails.[5] Let me look at each of these unworked machines in turn, in their echoing disconsonance.

The first paragraph of "*Die Sorge des Hausvaters*," strangely, discusses what contradictory things experts have had to say about the word or the name "Odradek." I say this is strange not only because a discussion of etymology is an odd way to begin a story or a confession, if it is either of these, but also because it is not at all evident how linguists have got hold of a word which appears to be a secret kept between Odradek and the *Hausvater*. Only now, it appears, is the father of the family revealing a secret that has been up to now apparently kept inside the house, so to speak. He conspicuously does not begin by saying, "I have submitted this name to linguists expert in etymologies, and here is what they say." Nevertheless, the word has apparently already been the subject of a lot of (fruitless) speculation. The *Hausvater*'s "cares" may have to do with his unsuccessful attempts to figure out, with the help of experts, what the word means. "No one," however, he says, "would occupy himself with such studies if there were not really a creature called Odradek." The *Hausvater* has Odradek in his care, at least during those times the strange animal-machine is roaming around the halls and stairways of his house or lurking in the attic. Therefore it is the house-father's care or *Sorge* to figure out what the creature's name means. Since Odradek, so far as I know, exists only in Kafka's text, I and other readers who have taken the word into their care are doing just what the *Hausvater* says no one in his or her right mind would do.

Nevertheless, linguists have got hold of the word somehow, says the *Hausvater*. Structural linguists and etymologists, we know, do not really care all that much about the existence or non-existence a word's referent. It is a word's putative meaning as an item in a network of differential relations to other words that interests them. Moreover, the linguists in this case disagree sharply. The speaker concludes, irrationally, from their inability to agree, that etymology is of no use in assigning meaning to the portentous sounding conglomeration of three syllables, "Odradek." "Some say," the little text begins, "that the word *Odradek* has roots in (*stamme aus*) the Slavic languages, and they attempt to demonstrate the formation (*Bildung*) of the word on that basis (*Grund*). Still others maintain that its roots are German, and that it is merely influenced by the Slavic" (72).

Somewhat unreasonably, the *Hausvater* concludes that this disagreement or uncertainty means that such researches are useless in finding a meaning for the word. Just because experts disagree, it seems to me, is no valid reason for giving up the search. "The uncertainty of both interpretations (*Deutungen*), however," says the text, "makes it reasonable to conclude that neither pertains, especially since neither of them enables you to find a meaning (*Sinn*) for the word" (72). I do not see how that uncertainty makes it reasonable to conclude any such thing. The *Hausvater*'s reasoning is as irrational as the word "Odradek." One or the other of the schools of linguists may be right. Nor does it rationally follow that trying out one or the other, or both, of the hypothesized roots might not reveal a plausible meaning for the word. What would forbid the word

"Odradek" from being a hybrid, like Kafka's disturbing kitten-lamb in "A Crossbreed," or like Kafka himself as a speaker of both German and Czech? "Odradek" may be a combination of Slavic and Germanic roots somewhat uneasily joined, with a fissure or fissures, perhaps a bottomless cloudy chasm,[6] opening up within the word, between its syllables or within them. Many such hybrid words do exist, for example in a polyglot or mongrel language like English.

What is at stake in this question of identifying meaning from etymons, however, as the reader will have noticed, is nothing less than the organic model as it dominates the traditional terminology of etymology, as in the term "word stem." The word "Odradek," experts claims, "has roots in" (*stamm aus*) either Slavic or German. One or the other of those languages is its "basis" (*Grund*). The word "Odradek" is rooted in the ground of either Slavic or German languages. The word has grown from them as a flower grows from its roots and stem.

The German word *Grund*, moreover, does not just mean "ground" in the "literal" sense of earth, garden soil. It is the German equivalent of the Greek *logos* or the Latin *ratio*. Latin *ratio* is affilated with *radius* and *radix*, root, as in our English word "radish," an edible root. Heidegger's book about the principle of reason is called *Der Satz vom Grund*. He follows Schopenhauer in making this translation of the Latin phrase *principium rationis*. As a translation of the Latin formula, the Leibnizian idea that everything has its reason, that reason can be rendered to everything, *der Satz vom Grund* sounds extremely odd to an English-speaker's ear. "Grund" for "reason"? That is not reasonable. It does not make sense.

"Etymon" comes from Greek *etumos*, true, real. The branch of linguistics called "etymology" is the search for the true original word from which later words are derived, as flower from root. The organic model, in this case, carries with it the whole system of Western metaphysics as embodied in that complex word, *logos*, meaning word, mind, ratio, rhythm, substance, ground, reason, and so on. In casually repudiating a procedure of reasoning out the meaning of the word "Odradek" by way of tracing its stem back to its roots in a grounded etymon, Kafka's speaker is rejecting the claim of that whole branch of linguistics to be able to identify true meaning: "neither of them [the two hypothesized language roots: Slavic,

German] enables you to find a meaning for the word" (*"man auch mit keiner von ihnen einen Sinn des Wortes finden kann"*) (72).

In spite of the speaker's firm prohibition, Kafka scholars from Max Brod to Werner Hamacher have not failed to take the bait. They have risen to the occasion. They have proposed all sorts of meanings for the separate syllables of the word "Odradek." These various meanings are to a considerable degree incompatible. Brod's essay containing his solution to the riddle of the word "Odradek" was already published in Kafka's lifetime. It presupposes Brod's characteristically religious reading of Kafka. Brod claims that the word "Odradek" contains "an entire scale of Slavic words meaning 'deserter' or 'apostate' . . . : deserter from the kind, *rod*; deserter from *Rat* (counsel), the divine decision about creation, *rada*." (qtd. in Hamacher 319). Brod puts this succinctly in another essay: "(Slavic etymology: having defected from counsel [*Rat*]—rada = Rat)" (Hamacher 319). Hamacher ironically wonders whether this reading of Odradek as meaning an apostate from the kind or *rod* says something about a man whose name was B*rod*. Wilhelm Emrich, in a book on Kafka of 1958, also cited by Hamacher, embroiders a bit on Brod's definition and secularizes it:

> In Czech [writes Emrich] . . . there is the verb *odraditi*, meaning to dissuade or deter someone from something. This word etymologically stems from the German (*rad* = *Rat*: advice, counsel, teaching). The subsequent Slavic "influence" is embodied in the prefix *od*, meaning *ab*, "off, away from," and in the suffix *ek*, indicating a diminutive. . . . Odradek . . . would therefore mean a small creature that dissuades someone from something, or rather, a creature that always dissuades in general. (qtd. in Hamacher 319-20)

That is all quite rational and clear. What Emrich says, however, does not jibe with what Brod says. For Brod, Odradek is in the condition of being an apostate. For Emrich, Odradek is someone who dissuades someone else from something. They cannot both be right. Moreover, neither Brod's meaning nor Emrich's is exemplified in the text itself. The *Hausvater*'s Odradek neither is shown to be an apostate from any faith, nor does he attempt to dissuade anyone, the *Hausvater* for example, from anything. Odradek just nimbly races up and down stairways, corridors, and halls, or lurks in the attic. These places are those inside/outside regions of a house or home that appear so often in Kafka's writings, for example as the locations of Joseph K.'s (almost) endlessly postponed trial in *The Trial*.

Werner Hamacher's own reading/non-reading of the word "Odradek" is by far the subtlest and most extensive I know. It goes on for pages. I cannot do justice to it here, but a sketch of what he says may be given. You must read Hamacher's essay for yourself. I identify three central features of what Hamacher says about "Odradek." 1) Hamacher is a distinguished master of what might be called paronomastics, the study of puns and wordplay, not the same as the science of word interpretation. Even the most apparently far-fetched associations are grist for Hamacher's mill, hay for his making. Hamacher makes a lot of hay. 2) The result is an amazing series of more or less contradictory words that Hamacher finds buried in "Odradek." If William Carlos Williams says a poem is "a small (or large) machine made of words" (256), Hamacher sees in "Odradek" one of those little unworked machines I am claiming is a new paradigm for thinking in many realms. The series Hamacher generates is like a forever incomplete set of variations on a few given sounds, like music by John Cage, John Adams, or Philip Glass, like a certain form of postmodern generative poetry, that by Georges Perec, John Cage, the Oulipo group,[7] or like some apparently mad sequence of superimposed words and phrases in *Finnegans Wake*,[8] or like the ones and zeroes in a computer file stored in the hard disk's random access memory, or like the just over three billions of DNA Base pairs in the human genome. The human genome is a huge set of permutations accumulated over millions of years, many of them meaningless or without apparent function. They are variations on a handful of basic letters naming chemical agglomerations. 3) Hamacher repeatedly insists that the upshot of this paronomastic investigation is not to identify the meaning, however complex, of the word "Odradek," but to confirm its lack of meaning or its paradoxical meaning as asserting that it is outside any meaning, that it means meaninglessness. Most etymologists agree that the first syllable, "od," is a privative, and that the last syllable, "ek," is a diminutive. The problem is the seemingly limitless plurivocity of the syllable "rad":

Any interpretation of "Odradek" that lays claim to certainty, conclusiveness, and meaning—and these are the hermeneutic principles of both "the family man" and the etymologists he criticizes—must miss "Odradek" because "Odradek" means dissidence, dissense, and a defection from the order of meaning. "Odradek" thus "means" that it does not mean. His discourse says that he denies this discourse, that he runs off course, that he de-courses; his name says that he has no name. (Hamacher 320-1)

Here is the strange Oulipian poem that emerges if I just run Hamacher's paronomastic word lists along in a row, with some of Hamacher's commentary interpolated. The reader will note that Hamacher takes away with one hand what he gives with the other. He wants to have these associations and at the same time to repudiate them as all false leads. The effect of the echoing potentially interminable series of words and word fragments is that they all gradually lose meaning and become mere sound, "rad, rad, rad, rad," in a crescendo of nonsense, as does the whole word "Odradek" if you repeat it often enough, as I am doing here, with Hamacher's help:

And among the uncertain meanings of "Odradek" which "the family man"—this economist of meaning who is always concerned with certainty in matters of interpretation—would have to refuse, there are also those that recall other connections in Czech: *rada* means not only *Rat* (counsel) but also series, row, direction, rank, and line; *rád* means series, order, class, rule as well as advisable, prudent; *rádek* means small series, row, and line. Odradek would thus be the thing that carried on its mischief outside of the linguistic and literary order, outside of speech, not only severed from the order of discourse (*Rede*) but also outside of every genealogical and logical series: a *Verräter*, a "betrayer" of every party and every conceivable whole.... Even the remark that "Odradek" can also be read as "Od-rade-K" and "Od-Rabe-K"—or "Od-raven-K"— and thus contains a double reference to the name "Kafka" [a favored move by Hamacher; he tends to see all Kafka's work as a hidden anagram of "Kafka" or "Franz Kafka," though he here rejects that move as illicitly explanatory] misses this "word," a word moving outside of the order of the word, outside of natural, national, and rational languages. Not even the name "Kafka," its contraction into the letter K, and its transformations into "jackdaw" and "raven" could be a source of meaning, an origin of discourse, or a root of reference, for "Kafka" separates itself in "Odradek" precisely from its roots, its *radix*. Odradek is the "od-radix": the one "without roots"; in Czech, *odrodek*, the one without its own kind, the one who "steps out of the lineage" (*odroditi*—to degenerate, to be uprooted). "Odradek" is, in short, the one who belongs to no kind and is without counsel, the one with neither a discourse nor a name of his own. . . . According to Kott's dictionary, *odraditi* means "to alienate," "to entice away"; *odranec* means "rags"; *odranka* means "a piece of paper," "patchwork of a text"; *odrati* means "tear off"; *odrbati* means "scrape off," "rub away"; *odrek* means "the renunciation"; *odrh* means "reproach," "reproof"; *odrod* and *odrodek* mean the one without a kind." Kafka may have connected pieces from all these with *Odradek*. They support the remark of Malcolm Paisley that Kafka would always speak of his writings as "patchwork," fragments soldered together, little bits of a story running around without a home (Hamacher 320-1).

If I abstract just the German, Czech, and Latin words from Hamacher's series I get the following Oulipian or Cagean more or less meaningless and unreadable poem. The individual items have meaning, but put together in this way, without grammar or syntax, they lose meaning and become variations on a mere sound or on possible ways of arranging a small selection of letters of the alphabet: *rada, Rat, rád, rádek, Rede, Verräter; ratio,* Od-rade-K, Od-Rabe-K, Od-raven-K, Kafka, *radix,* "od-radix"; *odrodek, odroditi, odraditi, odranec, odranka, odrati, odrbati, odrek, odrh, odrod, odrodek, Odradek.*

This string would be akin to the many unverifiable meanings that Jacques Derrida gives to the enigmatic phrase that starts his essay on "How to Avoid Speaking: Denials": "*Pardon de ne pas vouloir dire*" (which means, among other possibilities, "I beg your pardon for not wanting to speak," or "I beg your pardon for not meaning anything" (119-121; 161, 163**)), or to the variations in meaning that Thomas Pynchon, in one 221segment of *Gravity's Rainbow*, gives by changes in punctuation, emphasis, and context to a single word string "You never did the Kenosha Kid":

> Dear Mr. Slothrop:
> You never did.
>
> The Kenosha Kid. (62)
>
> Old veteran hoofer: Bet you never did the "Kenosha," kid! (62)
> You? Never! Did the Kenosha Kid think for one instant
>   that *you*...? (62)
> "You never did '*the,*' Kenosha Kid!" (62)
> But you never did the Kenosha kid. (63)
> You never did the Kenosha kid. Snap to, Slothrop. (63)
>   Voice: The Kid got busted. And you know me, Slothrop.
>   Remember? I'm Never.
>   Slothrop (peering): *You*, Never? (A pause.) *Did* the
>   Kenosha Kid? (72)

Another example would be the string of words, phonemes, and putative Indo-European roots in "g" that I spin out, with help from Derrida's *Glas*, in "Line," the first chapter of *Ariadne's Thread*: *graph, paragraph, paraph, epigraph, graffito, graft, graphium, graphion, graphein, gluphein, gleubh-, gher-, gerebh-, gno-, guh, gn, gl, gh, gr.* (9-10). Derrida's "Telepathy" appropriates another such multilingual string from Freud's strange essays on telepathy: "Forsyth . . . Forsyte, foresight, *Vorsicht, Vorasussicht*, precaution, or prediction [*prevision*]." Elsewhere in "Telepathy" Derrida appropriates a dazzling sequence, generated from the name "Claude" (ambiguously both male and female) from his own *Glas*: "*glas*... (*cla, cl, clos, lacs, le lacs, le piége, le lacet, le lais, là, da, fort, hum... claudication* [cla, cl, closed, lakes, snare, trap, lace, the silt, there, here, yes, away, hmmm ... limp])" (260-1, 234 (translation modified), 235; 269, 245, 246).[9] Other examples of such Oulipian poems can be found in the discussions of Cage, Perec, and Joyce in Louis Armand's "Constellations," referred to in note 8.

Given language systems or multiple interwoven language systems are non-rational assemblages in which the meaning of a given phoneme or string of phonemes may be apparently limited by context, by intonation, and by its difference from other phonemes or strings of phonemes. Nevertheless, a given string always exceeds its context and its differential limitations toward a limitless horizon of more and more remote but never entirely excludable puns, homonyms, and chance associations. The words or phrases in these lists are not ordered either by priority or temporally or as a narrative sequence. They could be given in any order. Implicitly they are simultaneous, like all the data in the Internet or like the items in a hypertext. The first item is not a beginning, nor is the last word an end. That makes Louis Armand's Mallarméan figure of the constellation appropriate, even though "constellation" implies a fixed pattern rather than the dynamically and unpredictably changing assemblage I am exemplifying here. The items in these sequences are like those bits of different colored thread knotted and twisted together that are wound on Odradek as if he were no more than a spool for saving used thread. Each list I have cited could be extended indefinitely in either direction. Ultimately, by a more and more outrageous process of substitution and permutation, such as Hamacher brilliantly deploys, as if he were a machine for making puns, any item, such as the "rad" in "Odradek," could lead to all the words in the Czeck and German languages, and to all the words in other languages too. It is no wonder sane people dislike puns and say of them what Samuel Johnson said: "He that would make a pun would pick a purse." Punning robs language of its rationality, as do the alliterations in Johnson's witty formulation. Paronomasia, like accidental alliterations, reveals that language is already an irrational machine. The will to meaning, the *"vouloir vouloir dire,"* can never capture or control this machine, anymore than the *Hausvater* can capture or control Odradek.

I have hypothesized that the thing that calls itself Odradek has an unstructuring structure that is analogous to the unworking (*désoeuvrant*) word-machine "Odradek." Let me be more specific about this. For one thing Odradek the thing is, like the word "Odradek," homeless. When the *Hausvater* asks Odradek where he lives, he says "No permanent residence (*Unbestimmter Wohnsitz*)" (73),[10] and then laughs. "But it is a kind of laughter that can only be produced without lungs. It sounds more or less like the rustling of fallen leaves (*wie das Rascheln in gefallenen Blättern*)" (73).

For me this is the most uncanny moment of "*Die Sorge des Hausvaters.*" It is akin to the skin-crawling and hair-raising moment when the Hunter Gracchus, who is caught permanently on his death-barge drifting between this world and the next, says: "My barge has no tiller, it is driven by the wind that blows in the nethermost regions of death" (*Kafka's Selected Stories* 112). Laughter is, experts claim, a form of distinctively human gesture-speech. We assume that animals cannot laugh. What, however, is laughter that is produced without lungs? It is laughter without laughter, an ironic undercutting of real laughter. Odradek's laughter is directed, oddly, toward the assertion that he has no permanent residence. It is an inhuman sound, like that produced by the rustling of fallen leaves. As Hamacher has recognized, however, "*Blättern*" is also the German word for the leaves of a printed book. Odradek's laughter, one might say, is a purely literary laughter. It is a sound generated by the words on the page and by their comparison with the sound of fallen leaves. But the leaves of this text are fallen, dead, dried out. They can only rustle. They are not legible and they cannot be read, like Odradek's laughter. Why does he laugh? No reason is given for why he finds having no permanent address risible. It hardly seems a laughing matter, or even an object fit for ironic non-laughing laughter.

The *Hausvater*'s description of Odradek the thing is as anomalous as the word that names him or it. Odradek is neither a human being, nor an animal, nor a thing, but rather a strange sort of talking and nimbly moving machine. Odradek is a (not very successful) robot, a technological construct that seems to have been made by someone not very good at designing robots. Or rather it is difficult to imagine that it had any designer at all. It seems to be the product of *techné* without a technician, as, it may, are the universe as a whole and human bodies within that universe, with their defective genomes, potentially self-destructive immune systems, and faulty endocrine systems. All three are prone to lethal non-working. We and our ecosystem may be the result of chance alterations over billions of years that have never yet quite got it right from the perspective of what we human beings think would be good for us.

Attractive as the argument from intelligent design is, since it gives a meaning to the creation and to all the creatures in it, the evidence strongly suggests that Darwin and recent physicists and geneticists are right: the universe and everything within it has evolved through billions of years of random variation, with the more or less random survival of the fittest determining which variations last longest. No rational designer could have put together the human genome, the endocrine system, and the immune system. Almost anyone could have done better than this *bricolage* of spare parts, with a lot of left-over parts (the nonsense sequences in the human genome) that do not seem to have any purpose or function at all. They may, however, have some hidden function that we have not yet identified, or may never be able to identify.

The same thing can be said of Odradek. The *Hausvater* says nothing at all about Odradek's genesis and genealogy. He seems to have no origin and no kin, to be *sui* generis, a one off, just as he seems to have no end in the sense of purpose or goal: "At first it looks like a flat, star-shaped spool for thread, and in fact, it does seem to be wound with thread; although these appear to be only old, torn-off pieces of thread of the most varied kinds and colors knotted together but tangled up in one another. But it is not just a spool, for a little crossbar sticks out from the middle of the star, and another little strut is joined to it at a right angle. With the help of this second little strut on the one side and one of the points of the star on the other, the whole thing can stand upright, as if on two legs" (72). If you try to imagine what this strange machine would look like, you have difficulty making sense of it. I never yet saw a spool for thread that was star-shaped, though commentators have seen a reference to the Star of David, first employed in Prague as a way of marking Jews. Nevertheless, how would you wind thread around the points of the star? In and out? They would slip off the star's points. The bits of thread are all tangled and knotted in any case, like those word and phoneme strings I discussed earlier. They have no apparent purpose beyond showing that Odradek or someone who uses him (it) is a thread-saver, though for no apparent reason. Perhaps some obscure reference may be encoded to Kafka's works as what he called a "patchwork" of narrative elements knotted together in a random sequence.

I can see how such an apparatus might stand upright, but I do not see how it can move so nimbly up and down the stairs, down the corridors, in the hallway, in the attic, as the *Hausvater* says it does. It is so extraordinarily mobile that it can never be caught: "*Odradek außerordentlich beweglich und nicht zu fangen ist.*" Though Odradek appears to be made of wood, it is self-propelled and it can speak and laugh, though it is without lungs. Like the kitten-lamb in "The Crossbreed," or the talking ape in "Report to an Academy," or like all those other talking and thinking animals in Kafka's work, Odradek belongs to no identifiable species. It is neither thing, nor plant, nor animal, nor human being, but a disturbing mixture of all these that defies reasonable classification.

The reader might be tempted to think that Odradek is incomplete, unfinished, or broken in some way, but the *Hausvater* says no proof of that exists, though he has sought evidence of it. If Odradek is incomplete and the missing parts could be found, then it might make better sense as a technological machine with some identifiable purpose: "It is tempting to think that this figure (*Gebilde*) once had some sort of functional shape {*zweckmäßige Form*] and is now merely broken. But this does not seem to be the case; at least there is no evidence for such a speculation; nowhere can you see any other beginnings or fractures that would point to anything of the kind; true, the whole thing seems meaningless yet in its own way complete (*das Ganze erscheint zwar sinnlos, aber in seiner Art abgeschlossen*)" (72). That would be a good description of Kafka's works, as well as of the paradigmatic Kafkesque word "Odradek." All these are complete, even the works he did not finish, but meaningless.

No wonder the *Hausvater* is worried. Kafka, I imagine, must have taken great delight in imagining a thing that would defy reasonable explanation, be meaningless, and yet "in its own way" complete, *abgeschlossen*, closed in on itself. He also must have enjoyed inventing a responsible and reasonable patriarch as "narrator" whose attempts to make sense of the creature that has invaded his household lead over and over to the verdict: "meaningless (*sinnlos*)," just as the name Odradek defies all attempts to give it a verifiable meaning. Both the name and the thing are cunning technological constructions whose "purpose" seems to be to defy reasonable explanation by human beings.

The final characteristic of Odradek is the one that causes the father of the family the most worry or *Sorge*. This is his fear that Odradek may be unable to die, again like the Hunter Gracchus. Anything mortal, the *Hausvater* says, has at least an identifiable goal, that is, to die. For Heidegger, an essential feature of *Daseins* is that they can foresee their death, as, according to him, animals cannot. *Sein zum Tode*, being toward death, is therefore what *Daseins* are. "Can he die?" asks the *Hausvater* about Odradek. "Everything that dies has previously had some sort of goal (*Ziel*), some kind of activity (*Tätigkeit*), and that activity is what has worn it down (*zerrieben*); this does not apply to Odradek" (73).

The principle of reason or *Satz vom Grund* that this strange little text radically puts in question presumes that anything with a rational meaning has that meaning because its activity is goal-oriented. Its meaning can be defined in terms of its goal or purpose, its *Zweck* or *Ziel*. Odradek has no goal and therefore his (its) activity does not wear him out until he (it) dies, as even a machine, however cleverly made, ultimately wears out. Only a technological construction without goal, purpose, or meaning can be immortal, perhaps like the universe itself in its endless movement of expansion and then contraction back to a new Big Bang. The *Hausvater*'s most haunting worry is that Odradek will outlive him and "that one day, with his bits of thread trailing behind him, he will come clattering down the stairs, at the feet of my children and my grandchildren[.] True, he clearly harms no one (*Er schadet ja offenbar niemandem*), but the idea that, on top of everything else, he might outlive me, that idea I find almost painful (*fast schmerzliche*)" (73).

After all this I have said about the word "Odradek" and the thing "Odradek" as a way of exemplifying the model of self-destructuring inorganic technological structures I have in mind as a replacement for thinking on the model of the organic, I can give short shrift,[11] or, to make a pun of my own, short *Schrift*, in the sense of just a few written words, to the two other forms of the inorganic machinal or technological this text exemplifies.

If "Odradek" is a word that is not a word and if Odradek it(him)self is a machine that is not a machine, *Die Sorge des Hausvaters* is an anomalous text that belongs to no recognizable genre. It is neither a story, nor a parable, nor an allegory, nor a confession, nor an autobiography, nor a scientific report, nor does it conform to the laws of any other recognized genre. It is an anomaly, an inorganic hybrid assemblage of words mixing aspects of many genres but conforming lawfully to none. It is not even much like other texts by Kafka. It is *sui generis*, a species with one exemplar, no parents and no offspring.

In a similar way, Die Sorge des Hausvaters does not create in the reader's mind the illusion of some recognizable character or personage. We learn little about the father of the family except that he is worried about Odradek. Kafka excels in creating a cool, slightly ironic, narrative voice that can hardly be called a "point of view," or a perspective, or either a reliable or an unreliable narrator, or the recognizable speech of a person. "*Die Sorge des Hausvaters*" is just a strange assemblage of words that seems to have fallen out of the sky, like a meteor, or like an inscribed astrolith, or like a scratched stone we might find on the beach. It just lies there like an indecipherable message in code. Though we know Kafka wrote it, nothing we can learn about Kafka the person explains or accounts for this fantastically inventive little text written in pellucid German. Its meaning is its successful resistance to interpretation, its failure to mean. It is *sinnlos*.

Whatever Works

Before turning to some present-day examples of destructuring structures, let me summarize the features of such a model as I have identified it in "*Die Sorge des Hausvaters.*" Such a technological artifact seems to have no creator. It seems to be self-generated and self-generating. It is certainly not the result of human will and technological knowhow. It is best described as a machine, but as machine that is unworked, inoperative, or disarticulated, though it goes on and on doing its thing, working away, like the Energizer bunny. It is *techné* without a technologist or technician, but a mad *techné* that produces machines that do not make sense from the perspective of human needs and wants, or from any other imaginable perspective.

I want in conclusion to set in parallel five systems that I claim are understandable, if they can be understood, according to the linguistico-machinal model I have sketched out, with Kafka's help: the environment, the global financial system, the nation-community, the body, and language. These mechanical sign-systems work. They make something happen, often in the end disaster from the human perspective. Each system can be seen as a figure for the others, but no one is the literal of which the others are displacements, figures, supplements, substitutions, or symbols. All are interconnected. Together they make an all-inclusive ecotechnological non-integrated whole into which each one of "us" is plugged.

One such system is terra, the earth. The earth, scientists are more and more discovering, is a complicated machine made of almost innumerable atoms and molecules that signal to one another. This machine is out of our control. It just goes on doing what it does do, that is, create the ever-changing climate within which we live, as in our environment, our house or *oikos*. The clever scientists, technicians, and engineers who invented and perfected the internal combustion engine that uses gasoline as a fuel, and then linked it to a vehicle with wheels, like the scientists who developed chemical fertilizers and pesticides, or coal-fired electrical plants, did not intend to cause catastrophic climate change. Nor did they at first know that, once started, climate change accelerates rapidly through feedback mechanisms. Scientists these days keep saying in amazement, "This is happening much faster than we thought it would!" The rapid increase of carbon dioxide and other green house gases in the atmosphere as a result of the later stages of industrialization has intervened in the ecosystem to trigger its self-modifying gears and levers. We intended no such thing, but that did not keep it from happening, mechanically.

The earth is not a super-organism. It is not an organism at all. It is best understood as an extremely complex machine that is capable of going autodestructively berserk, at least from the limited perspective of human needs. Global warming will bring about widespread species extinction. It will flood our low-lying islands, our coastal plains, and whatever towns, cities, and houses are on them. An example is our house on the shore of Deer Isle, Maine, where I am writing this, in sight of the ocean, only fifty feet away, its surface only a few feet down, at high tide, from the ground level of our house.

Moreover, as we continue to build up carbon in the atmosphere to higher and higher levels, we never know when the next emitted carbon-dioxide molecule will tip over some ecosystem and trigger a nonlinear climate event—like melting the Siberian tundra and releasing all its methane, or drying up the Amazon, or melting all the sea ice at the North Pole. The systems I am describing are best understood by way of chaos theory and catastrophe theory, that is, in terms of instantaneous breaks. Moreover, when one ecosystem collapses, it can trigger sudden unpredictable changes in others that could abruptly alter the whole earth (Friedman).

Another such machine is the global financial system. That machine is linked now to the Internet and to a host of computer-based data-storage and data-manipulation devices. Global capitalism in 2007 imploded, causing a worldwide recession and much human suffering. The unemployment level in the United States is at almost ten per cent, not counting the millions who have stopped looking for a job. The financiers, bankers, and CEOs whose decisions brought about this catastrophe did not intend to bring the financial system to the edge of total breakdown. Each acted rationally, so they thought, to maximize profits and garner their own high salaries, bonuses, and stock options. The financial meltdown happened, apparently, because too many people believed in the magic of a simple computer program formula that was supposed (falsely) to measure risk comparatively, i.e, the joint default probability of mortgages. David X. Li, then in Canada and the United States, but now back in Beijing, wrote the formula, a Gaussian copula formula of elegant simplicity (Salmon). The formula was fatally flawed by the assumption that house values would not, could not, go down. All the bankers and investment managers believed in that assumption, however, including the ratings agencies, paid by the financial "industry," that were giving AAA ratings to bundles of eventually almost totally worthless securities.

The computer programs "quants" devised allowed linked computers and databases to do things no human brain can understand. All the bankers and heads of financial institutions like Merrill Lynch, Bear Stearns, AIG, Citigroup, Bank of America, and so on, said, as their institutions were going belly up, that they did not understand what a credit default swap is, or what a CDO (collateralized debt obligation) is, or just what are the workings of programs that make tranches and tranches of tranches to distribute subprime mortgages into more and more remote slices. This procedure was supposed to spread the risk so widely that no one would suffer appreciable loss if someone defaulted on one of the mortgages. Those in charge of banks and financial companies were not lying when they said they did not know how far in debt they were. It appears that many were totally insolvent. One hundred and four smaller banks failed in the United States by October 24, 2009, and bank failures have continued worldwide since then. CDO's added up to $4.7 trillion in 2006. By 2007 the amount of credit default swaps (CDSs) outstanding was the astounding sum of $62 trillion. The banks and financial companies were destroyed, or would have been destroyed if they had not been saved by a massive infusion of billions of dollars of taxpayers' money, by something built into the system that was not an object of cognition, though some whistle-blowers put up warning signs. This is a little like the way I do not understand just what is going on somewhere deep inside my computer when I press certain little keys on my keyboard and get this present sentence on my screen in twelve point Palatino, double-spaced, with certain pre-set margins and other automatic formatting. Our cats are adept at accidentally pressing fortuitous combinations of keys that cause my laptop to "crash," just as the stock market crashed. Like the CEOs already mentioned, in relation to their highly paid computer quants, I have no idea just what my cats have done, nor how to undo it.

It is an essential feature of the modern financial system that it depends on computer programs and elaborately interconnected computers for its workings. These workings exceed human comprehension. That does not, however, keep them from going on doing their thing, in what might be called by anthropomorphism a revenge of the robots. The unexpectedly accelerated pace of global warming and species extinction is parallel to this unknowabilty of the workings of the financial system. Experts have to keep revising the time frame for the inundation of our Deer Isle house. It keeps getting more and more imminent. "Get ready! The end of the world is at hand!" "Get ready! The financial system is in meltdown!" It will not have escaped my reader's notice that "meltdown" and "toxic," as in "toxic assets," are terms borrowed from the vocabulary of climate change. Thomas Friedman, in the New York Times Op Ed column cited above, expresses our inadvertently-caused plight as follows:

> To recover from the Great Recession, we've had to go even deeper into debt. One need only look at today's record-setting price of gold, in a period of deflation, to know that a lot of people are worried that our next dollar of debt— unbalanced by spending cuts or new tax revenues—will trigger a nonlinear move out of the dollar and torpedo the U.S. currency.
>
> If people lose confidence in the dollar, we could enter a feedback loop, as with the climate, whereby the sinking dollar forces up interest rates, which raises the long-term cost of servicing our already massive debt, which adds to the deficit projections, which further undermines the dollar. If the world is unwilling to finance our deficits, except at much higher rates of interest, it would surely diminish our government's ability to make public investments and just as surely diminish our children's standard of living.
>
> As the environmentalist Rob Watson likes to say, "Mother Nature is just chemistry, biology and physics. That's all she is. You can't spin her; you can't sweet-talk her. You can't say, 'Hey, Mother Nature, we're having a bad recession, could you take a year off?'" No, she's going to do whatever chemistry, biology and physics dictate, based on the amount of carbon we put in the atmosphere, and as Watson likes to add: "Mother Nature always bats last, and she always bats a thousand."

[Addendum 11/29/11: Friedman's scenario of self-destructive high interest rates has not taken place yet in the United States, but just this event has recently occurred in the "Club-Med" nations of the Euro-zone that are on the verge of bankruptcy: Greece, Ireland, Italy, Spain, Portugal. Both the Euro-zone nations and the United States, however, are making the same disastrous ideological (that is, robot-like) mistake of thinking they can return to economic well-being by slashing government spending and lowering taxes on the rich and on big corporations. This is exactly the wrong thing to do, as Ireland's present plight demonstrates. Following this strategy would be a catastrophe eventually even for the rich and for corporations because it would greatly reduce the income consumers must have to buy the goods corporations make. Meanwhile, unemployment in the United States remains at over nine percent (much higher if you count those who are underemployed or who have stopped looking for a job); hundreds of thousands of people are losing their houses through mortgage foreclosures, some illegal; the top 1% of Americans make 20% of the national income and control 40% of the nation's wealth; national health care costs are rising to 20% of GDP and will go on rising; soaring tuition costs are putting higher education out of the reach of more and more Americans, in a litany of interlocked auto-co-immune disasters.]

The third such system is a community or a nation. Such a construct is an interrelated conglomeration of human beings controlled by laws, institutions, constitutions, legislatures, and all the machinery of government, what Foucault calls "governmentality." The financial system is an important part of a given national fabric, especially in a militarist-capitalist-teletechnoscientific plutocracy like the United States. What is most conspicuous about the United States today, if we think of it not as an organism but as a technological artifact, a product of *techné*, is its penchant for mindless or at least irrational self-destruction.

Why is it that a large group of apparently well-meaning and apparently sane human beings are hell-bent on auto-destruction? The best description of this I know is Jacques Derrida's hypothesis of what he calls "auto-co-immunity," that is, a penchant within any community that turns its forces against itself. Such a community destroys itself by way of what is intended to make it safe, whole, indemnified from harm, just as auto-immunity in the human body's immune system turns the body against itself. I have discussed Derrida's "auto-co-immunity" at some length in *For Derrida* (123-9), but here are the essential passages, from Derrida's "Faith and Knowledge" and "Rogues." They speak for themselves:

> But the auto-immunitary haunts the community and its system of immunitary survival like the hyperbole of its own possibility. Nothing in *common*, nothing immune, safe and sound, *heilig* and holy, nothing unscathed in the most autonomous living present without a risk of auto-immunity.... This excess above and beyond the living, whose life only has absolute

value by being worth more than life, more than itself—this, in short, is what opens the space of death that is linked to the automaton (exemplarily "phallic"), to technics, the machine, the prosthesis, virtuality: in a word, to the dimensions of the auto-immune and self-sacrificial supplementarity, to this death drive that is silently at work in every community, every *auto-co-immunity*, constituting it in truth as such in its iterability, its heritage, its spectral tradition. Community as *com-mon auto-immunity*: no community <is possible> that would not cultivate its own auto-immunity, a principle of sacrificial self-destruction ruining the principle of self-protection (that of maintaining its self-integrity intact), and this in view of some sort of invisible and spectral sur-vival. This self-contesting attestation keeps the auto-immune community alive, which is to say, open to something other and more than itself: the other, the future, death, freedom, the coming or the love of the other, the space and time of a spectralizing messianicity beyond all messianism. It is there that the possibility of religion persists: the religious bond (scrupulous, respectful, modest, reticent, inhibited) between the value of life, its absolute "dignity," and the theological machine, the "machine for making gods. (82, 87 [translation slightly modified]); original 62, 68-9).

Yet all these efforts to attenuate or neutralize the effect of the traumatism (to deny, repress, or forget it, to get over it [*pour en faire son deuil*], etc.) are, they also, but so many desperate attempts. And so many autoimmunitary movements. Which produce, invent, and feed the very monstrosity they claim to overcome.

What will never let itself be forgotten is thus the perverse effect of the autoimmunitary itself. For we now know that repression in both its psychoanalytical sense and its political sense—whether it be through the police, the military, or the economy [*au sens politico-policier, politico-militaire, politico-économique*]—ends up producing, reproducing, and regenerating the very thing it seeks to disarm (99 [translation slightly modified]; original 152).

The Patriot Act and the Department of Homeland Security have made United States citizens conspicuously less safe by taking away our precious civil liberties, subjecting us to universal surveillance and the danger of indefinite imprisonment, perhaps by way of "extraordinary rendition," to be tortured in a secret prison in a foreign country. I identify in iteration in variation four further regions where the United States is currently engaged in auto-immune self-destruction.

One, perhaps the worst, is the refusal to have done anything serious about global climate change until it is already too late. It is already too late, I mean, to keep the atmospheric temperature and the ocean levels from rising to levels that will make the planet in most places uninhabitable.

Another auto-immune gesture is the refusal to do anything serious to regulate the financial system. Bankers and investment officials are already returning to their old ways of excessive risk-taking along with setting outrageous salaries and bonuses for themselves. Banks and investment houses are fighting tooth and nail to keep regulation from happening. This is perhaps because they secretly know that climate change will cause devastation. They know what they are doing will cause another financial meltdown, but are squirreling away huge sums of money so they can pay to be part of the surviving remnant living in gated communities perched high above the rising waters. Or so they imagine.

A third example of auto-immune behavior is the refusal even to consider the only rational solution to our catastrophic health-care system, namely single payer government-run health care. The Republicans have sworn to repeal the modest and not very effective health care bill that was passed when Democrats still controlled both houses of Congress. They also want to eviscerate Medicare and Medicaid, which would cause tens of thousands of our citizens to die from lack of adequate healthcare, in a perhaps not entirely undeliberate process of population culling. It is difficult to believe that the Republicans, some of them at least, do not know what they are doing. Without a robust so-called "public option" the "reforms" that passed Congress and was signed by Presideny Obama will only make the health care insurance companies and the pharmaceutical companies immensely richer, costing far beyond the current sixteen to twenty per cent of the Gross Domestic Product that we spend on health care in the United States.

A fourth example, also already mentioned, is the delay in withdrawing from the war in Afghanistan and bringing our troops home. Trillions of taxpayer dollars have already been sunk into the wars of occupation in Iraq and Afghanistan, not to speak of the human toll in killed and wounded on all sides.

If you just stand back a little and look at these four problems, it is easy to see the rational solutions. Our collective auto-co-immunity, however, seems to make it extremely unlikely that any of these solutions will be chosen. Apparently we will remain blindly bent on self-destruction.

An additional realm of the technological is the "human being," thought of as soul embodied, material spirit. The body is now more and more seen as not organic in the warm fuzzy sense we have tended to mean that, but as a complex product of *techné*, with the universe as ecotechnician. The human immune system is exemplary of the body's machine-like self-functioning, as is the endocrine system. You cannot direct your antibodies to do this or that by thinking about them. They act on their own. It is *L'homme machine*, as de la Mettrie said, or *La femme machine*, but with a tendency to self-destruction built in. Hypothyroidism is, for example, apparently an autoimmune disease, as is, perhaps, pancreatic cancer, and as are many other diseases and cancers. Many forms of cancer appear to be brought about by random mishaps in the genetic code. We cannot influence by thinking the way a string of genetic code generates a certain protein or enzyme, as it is programmed to do, or the way the immune system produces antibodies against what it perceives, not always correctly, as invading alien antigens. These mechanical systems do not always work all that well. They are cumbersome, redundant, and prone to error. Recent work on the human genome and its functions, on cell biology, on the endocrine system, on the immune system with its terrifying power of self-destructive autoimmunity, and by neuroscientists on brain chemistry and the brain's "wiring" is showing that a technological paradigm is a better way than a traditional organic paradigm to understand the body and even its most human-appearing concomitants of consciousness and the accompanying senses of self-hood and volition.

An authoritative recent feature essay in *Science News*, "Enter the Virosphere," summarizes recent work on viruses in ways that indicate how the workings of genes are machine-like, but make big problems for assumptions about what constitutes "life." Viruses were thought not to be alive, but scientists are now increasingly not so sure, hence the pun in the title "Virosphere" rather than "Biosphere." On the one hand, viruses do not eat, respire, or reproduce. They have no metabolism, so they must be dead. On the other hand, viruses are made of genetic material that acts in many ways like that in "living organisms" such as bacteria, algae, rabbits, and human beings. A gene is a gene. Whether a given gene is in a virus or in the human genome, it is a pattern that constructs things like proteins. Viruses are everywhere. "A thimbleful of sea water contains millions of virus particles" (Ehrenberg 22). Viruses make up about 90 percent of the ocean's biomass, killing an estimated 20 percent of that biomass every day. "Their killing feeds the world" (22), since so many "organisms" feed on dead organisms killed by viruses. Just as a living cell's nucleus uses its surrounding cytoplasm "to replicate its own DNA using machinery outside of itself" (qtd. from Jean-Michel Claverie in Ehrenberg 25), a virus is made of genetic material that acts like a nucleus in entering a host cell and using the machinery of that cell to reproduce itself. Viruses borrow genes from other gene systems and either pass them on to "infect" other gene systems, or incorporate them in their own genomes.

It might be best to say that the new evidence does not so much lead to the conclusion that viruses are alive as suggest that all so-called living things are subject, like viruses, to the machine-like processes of gene action. It may even be that the first "living thing" was a protovirus that ultimately mutated into biological cells, though that hypothesis is highly controversial. It might aid coming to terms with "*Die Sorge des Hausvaters*" if we think of Odradek as virus-like, or at any rate of we include the virus along with thing, plant, animal, and human beings in Odradek's hybrid mixture of language-like systems. The virus's relation to language is indicated in the terminology used to describe the two different ways bacterial and animal viruses enter a host cell, replicate themselves, and then leave the cell to continue their work. This is often a work of killing. According to how virologists express this process, the viral genome enters a cell, "replicates" itself, then "transcribes" itself," then "translates" itself, finally "assembling" and "packaging" itself before the replicated viral genome exits the cell in new multiple copies, like those made by a copying machine.

Figures drawn from the workings of language are, you can see, essential to expressing the results of genetic research. The three dominant metaphors in Ehrenberg's article are "machinery," "language," and "infection." These are used unselfconsciously and unproblematically. They are the usual figurative words for the way a virus works. One paragraph, however, ostentatiously, with evident irony, uses a sustained metaphor comparing the way viruses work to the global financial system, with sinister implications for the mindless technicity of both. The paragraph also reinforces my claim that we tend to think of each of these systems by figurative analogy with the others, in the absence of any grounded literal terminology. Any description of these products of *techné* is catachrestic, that is, the borrowing from one realm of a term then used to name something whose working has no satisfactory literal name: "Viruses also may keep genes they've procured, and even bundle these assets together, as appears to be the case with several photosynthesis genes recently found in marine viruses. These findings hint at the vast viral contribution to the ocean's gross national product and viruses' significance in global energy production" (22).

Fifth: Textual systems, sign systems generally, are also machine-like in their action. This can best be seen in the interference of constative and performative forms of language. Once these systems come into being (who knows how?) they are out of our control. They do things on their own which we are powerless to stop. As Paul de Man argued, we cannot prevent ourselves from making the same errors of misreading all over again even when we have correctly identified them as errors.[12] Decisive here is de Man's idea that performative utterances work on their own, not as a result of human agency. They work mechanically, through the force of language. And they work in weird and unpredictable ways. De Man always emphasized the mechanical, non-human, and arbitrary workings of language, as does, in a somewhat different way, Louis Armand throughout *Literate Technologies*.[13] The first draft of the present essay was written by way of examples that were accessed spontaneously and somewhat randomly from the database stored somewhere in my brain's memory center. Sentences just formed themselves magically in my mind, as words were fitted into pre-existing grammatical and syntactical paradigms. This happened by a process of invention in the double sense of discovery and making up. I then typed these sentences into my laptop. I suppose most writing by anyone gets done that way. It is uneasy-making, however, to realize that writing is so little under the writer's conscious control and volition. I never know what I am going to write until I write it. *Die Sprache spricht:* Language speaks. It speaks through me by a species of ventriloquism that uses me (in the sense of my body and my computer literate, keyboard-tapping, conscious self and fingers) as medium.

For Paul de Man, a performative utterance makes something happen, but not what is intended or predicted. The last sentences of de Man's "Promises (*Social Contract*)" express this in terms of that paradigmatic performative, a promise: "The redoubtable efficacy of the text is due to the rhetorical model of which it is a version. This model is a fact of language over which Rousseau himself has no control. Just as any other reader, he is bound to misread his own text as a promise of political change. The error is not within the reader; language itself dissociates the cognition from the act. *Die Sprache verspricht (sich)*; to the extent that is necessarily misleading, language just as necessarily conveys the promise of its own truth" (de Man 277). The German phrase is an ironic allusion to Heidegger's portentous, *Die Sprache spricht*, "Language speaks," cited earlier. "*Versprechen*" means "to promise," as a reflexive: "to promise itself," but it also means "to make a slip of the tongue." This happens because of the doubleness of the prefix "*ver-*," which can mean both for and against. De Man's little phrase is an example of the nonsensical paronomasias, puns, and wordplay, built mechanically into language. Language speaks all right, but it says things the speaker does not intend, that are *necessarily* misleading, for example in the form of a promise that cannot be kept. De Man goes on, notoriously, to assert that such rhetorical complexities, such linguistic mixups, "generate history." As de Man expressed this unsettling feature of performative language in a graduate seminar: "you aim at a bear and an innocent bird falls out of the sky."

Put these five domains together, working like the interconnected machines that they are, linked as one big and extremely cumbersome and *désoeuvrée* machine, and you get the revolt of the robots big time.

Using the technological model as a way of outlining what is happening in these five realms will not keep what is occurring from occurring. Like Odradek, my prime model in this essay of the inorganic ecotechnological, these unworked machines just keep on mindlessly doing their thing. This alternative paradigm does, however, provide a better *techné* or tool than the organic model for sketching out what is happening as the water rises around us. Unfortunately, however, as my emphasis on what is irrational or aporetic about the (non)machines of various sorts I have named, the ecotechnological model does not lead to clear cognition or understanding. At most it invites the sorts of performative action, such as passing laws about carbon emissions, that seem exceedingly unlikely to take place. The implacable law of auto-co-immunity forbids that.

This failure of both cognition and of effective action is taking place in fulfillment of a weird translation into Mayan hieroglyphs of Christ's words on the cross. The oral expressions of these hieroglyphs were then transliterated into Western letters, according to a perhaps fallacious mystery story I can no longer find among our books: "Sinking, Sinking! Black ink over nose." This essay might be thought of as the inscription in black ink, exemplifications of the technicity of the letter, written on the nose of someone drowning in black ink.

Notes

1. See Heidegger's *An Introduction to Metaphysics* 45-50 (original 34-8).

2. See Werner Hamacher, "The Gesture in the Name: On Benjamin and Kafka," in *Premises: Essays on Philosophy and Literature from Kant to Celan.*, trans. Peter Fenves (Cambridge, MA: Harvard University Press, 1996), especially 296-300.

3. For a fuller discussion, see my *The Medium is the Maker: Browning, Freud, Derrida and the New Telepathic Ecotechnologies* (Brighton and Portland: Sussex Academic Press, 2009).

4. This the complex word Jean-Luc Nancy uses in the title of his book about modern non-community communities: *The Inoperative Community* (*La communauté désoeuvrée*). *The Inoperative Community*, ed. Peter Connor, trans. Connor, Lisa Garbus, Michael Holland, and Simona Sawney (Minneapolis: University of Minnesota Press, 1991).

5. The metaphor of a "cloudy spot" in Kafka's writings, especially the parables, occurs three times in Walter Benjamin's great "Kafka" essay. Of the opening anecdote about Potemkin, Benjamin says "The enigma which beclouds this story is Kafka's enigma" (795). The famous parable "Before the Law" has a "cloudy spot at its interior" (802), and Kafka's use of gesture is said to form "the cloudy part of the parables" (808). This part is cloudy because it is the place where clear-seeing of the doctrine, teaching, or moral that the parable ought to express is impossible. The parables of Jesus have a clear meaning. The parable of the sower in Matthew is about the Kingdom of Heaven and how to get there. Jesus tells the disciples that this is the case. Kafka's parables have no such identifiable meaning. An impenetrable opacity resides where the meaning ought to be. Kafka's parables therefore mean their lack of identifiable meaning.

6. My allusion is to what Walter Benjamin says of Kafka's parables. See previous footnote.

7. "Oulipo (French pronunciation: [ulipo], short for French: *Ouvroir de littérature potentielle*; roughly translated: 'workshop of potential literature') is a loose gathering of (mainly) French-speaking writers and mathematicians which seeks to create works using constrained writing techniques. It was founded in 1960 by Raymond Queneau and François Le Lionnais. Other notable members include novelists Georges Perec and Italo Calvino, poet Oskar Pastior and poet/mathematician Jacques Roubaud. The group defines the term *'littérature potentielle'* as (rough translation): 'the seeking of new structures and patterns which may be used by writers in any way they enjoy.' Constraints are used as a means of triggering ideas and inspiration, most notably Perec's 'story-making machine' which he used in the construction of *Life: A User's Manual*. As well as established techniques, such as lipograms (Perec's novel *A Void*) and palindromes, the group devises new techniques, often based on mathematical problems such as the Knight's Tour of the chessboard and permutations" ("Oulipo"). Wikipedia, <http://en.wikipedia.org/wiki/Oulipo>. [Accessed Nov. 5, 2011.])

8. For Cage, Perec, Oulip, and Joyce as creators of texts in one way or another made by a machine-like process of permutation see the brilliantly learned and provocative book by Louis Armand, *Literate Technologies: Language, Cognition, Technicity*, especially the final chapter, "Constellations," 165-223. Though Armand's primary focus is on the technological aspects of language, thought, and consciousness, what he calls "literate technologies," rather than on climate change, on the financial system, or on national communities, or even on the effects of new media, his book has nevertheless greatly influenced my thinking in this essay.

9. I have discussed these sequences in *The Medium is the Maker*, 27-9.

10. For whatever it is worth, which is probably not much, Kafka himself had no permanent residence. Guides to Prague visitors, as I know from experience, point out apartment after apartment where Kafka is said to have lived, mostly with his family, if what he did can be called living, which Kafka himself doubted. Most of these apartments are around the famous Old Town Square or on adjacent side streets, but at least one is in a quite different part of the city, across the river and near Prague Castle. Like Joyce in Zurich, Kafka moved a lot. He was without permanent residence. Joyce moved from flat to flat because he could not pay his rent and was evicted. Kafka moved because his father was rising up in the world and wanted to live in always more and more pretentious apartments.

11. A "shrift" is a penalty prescribed to a Catholic parishioner by a priest after confession. Criminals sentenced to be hanged were given "short shrift" before being executed. They were shriven in a hurry. See Shakespeare, Richard III. "To give him short shrift" is in German *"kurzen Prozeß mit ihm machen."* *Prozeß* is certainly a word with Kafkaesque resonances, though Joseph K's *Prozeß* is anything but short. He is told rather that his best hope is to make his trial interminable, which, unhappily, does not happen.

12. See de Man's "Allegory of Reading (Profession de foi)" in *Allegories of Reading* (New Haven: Yale University Press, 1979): "Deconstructive readings can point out the unwarranted identifications achieved by substitution, but they are powerless to prevent their recurrence even in their own discourse, and to uncross, so to speak, the aberrant exchanges that have taken place" (242).

13. See, for example, de Man's "Excuses (Confessions)" in *Allegories of Reading*: "The deconstruction of the figural dimension is a process that takes place independently of any desire; as such it is not unconscious but mechanical, systematic in its performance but arbitrary in its principle, like a grammar. This threatens the autobiographical subject not as the loss of something that once was present and that it once possessed, but as a radical estrangement between the meaning and the performance of any text" (298).

Works Cited

Armand, Louis. *Literate Technologies: Language, Cognition, Technicity.* Prague: Literaria Pragensia, 2006.

Benjamin, Walter. "Franz Kafka: On the Tenth Anniversary of His Death." *Selected Writings: Volume 2: 1927-1934.* Trans. Rodney Livingstone. Ed. Michael W. Jennings, Howard Eiland, and Gary Smith. Cambridge, MA: The Belknap Press of Harvard University Press, 1999.

de Man, Paul. *Allegories of Reading.* New Haven: Yale University Press, 1979.

Derrida, Jacques. "Literature in Secret: An Impossible Filiation." *The Gift of Death*. 2nd ed. Trans. David Wills. Chicago: University of Chicago Press, 2008. Trans. of "*La littérature au secret: Une filiation impossible*." *Donner la mort*. Paris: Galilée, 1999.

———. "Telepathy." Trans. Nicholas Royle. *Psyche: Inventions of the Other, Volume I*. Ed. Peggy Kamuf and Elizabeth Rottenberg. Stanford: Stanford University Press, 2007. Trans. of "Télépathie." *Psyché: Inventions de l'autre*. Paris: Galilée, 1987.

———. "Faith and Knowledge: The Two Sources of 'Religion' at the Limits of Reason Alone." Trans. Samuel Weber. *Acts of Religion*. Ed. Gil Anidjar. New York and London: Routledge, 2002. Trans. of "Foi et savoir: Les deux sources de la 'religion' aux limites de la simple raison." *La religion*, with Gianni Vattimo. Ed. Thierry Marchaisse. Paris: Seuil, 1996.

———. "Autoimmunity: Real and Symbolic Suicides." *Philosophy in a Time of Terror: Dialogues with Jürgen Habermas and Jacques Derrida*, with Jürgen Habermas and Giovanna Borradori. Chicago: University of Chicago Press, 2003. Trans. of *Le 'concept' du 11 septembre: Dialogues à New York (octobre-décembre 2001)*. With Jürgen Habermas and Giovanna Borradori. Paris: Galilée, 2004.

Ehrenberg, Rachel. "Enter the Virosphere." *Science News*. 10 Oct. 2009. 22-25.

Friedman, Thomas. "Our Three Bombs." *New York Times*. 6 Oct. 2009. Web. 7 Oct. 2009. <http://www.nytimes.com/2009/10/07/opinion/07friedman.html?th&emc=th>. (Accessed Nov. 5, 2011.)

Hamacher, Werner. "The Gesture in the Name: On Benjamin and Kafka." *Premises: Essays on Philosophy and Literature from Kant to Celan*. Trans. Peter Fenves. Cambridge, MA: Harvard University Press, 1996.

Heidegger, Martin. *Being and Time*. Trans. John Macquarrie and Edward Robinson. London: SCM Press, 1962. Trans. of *Sein und Zeit*. Tübingen: Max Niemeyer, 1967.

———. *The Fundamental Concepts of Metaphysics: World, Finitude, Solitude*. Trans. William McNeill and Nicholas Walker. Bloomington: Indiana University Press, 1995. Trans. of *Die Grundbegriffe der Metaphysik*. Frankfurt am Main: Vittorio Klostermann, 1983.

———. *An Introduction to Metaphysics*. Trans. Ralph Manheim. New Haven: Yale University Press, 1959. Trans. of *Einführung in die Metaphysik*. Tübingen: Max Niemeyer, 1966.

———. "Language." *Poetry, Language, Thought*. Trans. Albert Hofstadter. New York: Harper and Row, 1971. Trans. of "Die Sprache." *Unterwegs zur Sprach*. Pfullingen: Neske, 1959.

Kafka, Franz. "The Worry of the Father of the Family." *Kafka's Selected Stories*. Ed. and trans. Stanley Corngold. New York: W.W. Norton, 2007. 72-3. Trans. of "*Die Sorge des Hausvaters.*" <http://www.kafka.org/index.php?landarzt>. (Accessed Nov. 5, 2011.)

Miller, J. Hillis. *Ariadne's Thread*. New Haven: Yale University Press, 1992.

———. *For Derrida*. New York: Fordham University Press, 2009.

———. *The Medium is the Maker: Browning, Freud, Derrida and the New Telepathic Ecotechnologies*. Brighton and Portland: Sussex Academic Press, 2009.

Nancy, Jean-Luc. *Corpus*. Paris: Métailié, 2006.

———. *The Inoperative Community*. Ed. Peter Connor. Trans. Connor, Lisa Garbus, Michael Holland, and Simona Sawney. Minneapolis: University of Minnesota Press, 1991. Trans. of *La communauté désoeuvrée*. Paris: Christian Bourgois, 2004.

"Oulipo." Wikipedia. Web. 25 Oct. 2009. <http://en.wikipedia.org/wiki/Oulipo>. (Accessed Nov. 5, 2011.)

Pynchon, Thomas. *Gravity's Rainbow*. New York: Penguin, 1973.

Ruskin, John. "Of the Pathetic Fallacy." <http://www.ourcivilisation.com/smartboard/shop/ruskinj/>. (Accessed Nov. 5, 2011.)

Salmon, Felix. "A Formula for Disaster." *Wired*. March 2008. 74+.

Williams, William Carlos. *Selected Essays*. New York: Random House, 1954.

V

Theories of Community
Nancy Contra Stevens

Le témoignage le plus important et le plus pénible du monde moderne, celui qui rassemble peut-être tous les autres témoignages que cette époque se trouve chargée d'assumer, en vertu d'on ne sait quel décret ou de quelle nécessité (car nous témoignons aussi de l'épuisement de la pensée de l'Histoire), est le témoignage de la dissolution, de la dislocation ou de la conflagration de la communauté.

Jean-Luc Nancy, *La communauté désoeuvrée*[1]

The gravest and most painful testimony of the modern world, the one that possibly gathers together all other testimonies which this epoch finds itself charged with assuming, by virtue of who knows what decree or necessity [for we bear witness also to the exhaustion of thinking by way of History], is the testimony of the dissolution, the dislocation, or the conflagration of community.

Jean-Luc Nancy, *The Inoperative Community*[2]

We were as Danes in Denmark all day long
And knew each other well, hale-hearted landsmen,
For whom the outlandish was another day

Of the week, queerer than Sunday. We thought alike
And that made brothers of us in a home
In which we fed on being brothers, fed

And fattened as on a decorous honeycomb.
This drama that we live—We lay sticky with sleep.
Wallace Stevens, "The Auroras of Autumn"[3]

This chapter builds on recent theoretical investigations of community to establish a set of tentative hypotheses for my investigations of community's conflagration in fiction before and after Auschwitz. The chapter juxtaposes or "compears" two quite different models of community. "Compear" is "a legal term that is used to designate appearing before a judge together with another person."[4] The word will come up again later in this chapter as a translation of Jean-Luc Nancy's word "*comparution*." My setting side by side, as if haled before a tribunal, of two concepts of community will provide a somewhat uneasy foundation for my investigation of community or the lack of it in some novels written before and after the Holocaust.

My initial citation is the first sentence from one of many recent philosophical or theoretical works that have reflected on what is meant by the word "community" and on what has happened to community in modern times.[5] What Nancy says is peculiar in several ways. For one thing, he starkly opposes giving testimony and clear knowledge, such as historians are supposed to supply. Witnessing is a speech act, a performative enunciation, while "*la pensée de l'Histoire*" ("the thinking according to History") leads to constative statements. These are statements of facts that are verifiable as true or false. We can bear witness to what has happened to community in modern times—its dissolution, dislocation, or conflagration. We cannot know it or understand it. We have to accept the burden of testifying to the conflagration of community, but we must do that by virtue of some unknown decree or necessity. Someone or something has decreed our painful obligation to bear witness to the end of community, but who or what has done that is "unknown." Even the decree itself is "unknown," though it obliges us implacably. We are obligated by a decree whose exact formulation and whose source of authority we cannot know.

That is exceedingly strange, if you think of it. What does it mean to be coerced by a decree or law whose wording we cannot know? Ignorance of the law is no excuse, but, still, it is unpleasant, to say the least, to be subject to a decree of which we must remain ignorant. It is a little like Joseph K.'s experience, in Kafka's *The Trial*, of being arrested one fine day even though he has not done anything wrong. Playing a little on the word "trial," one could even translate Nancy's assertion that we are *"chargée d'assumer"* ("charged with taking on") this painful testimony by saying such bearing witness is a trial we must endure, even though we are not aware of having done anything wrong. This bearing witness, Nancy assures us, is so important and so painful (*"penible"*) that it seems as if it possibly involves all the other responsibilities of witnessing to which we in the modern world are subject.

A further peculiarity of Nancy's sentence is that it contradicts itself. It exemplifies the thinking by way of History that, at the same moment, it says is exhausted. The passage implies that once community existed, but now, in the modern world, community has been dissolved, dislocated, or conflagrated. Something had to be there initially to suffer those transformations. That is a historical proposition if there ever was one. It is a statement capable of being true or false. Nancy's book as a whole, moreover, contradicts this historical proposition. It does so by expressing, as is characteristic of Western philosophical thinking, its definition of an "inoperative community" as a universal human condition. Nancy's propositions, his way of stating his assertions implies, are true in all places, in all cultures, and at all times.

La communauté désoeuvrée as a whole deconstructs, if I may dare to use that word, its strikingly apodictic first sentence. A thesis/antithesis with no possible sublation, a suspended or hovering self-canceling, bears witness to the way any thought of the dissolution of community depends on the traditional idea of community it would put in question. In a reciprocal way, the traditional concept of community, as expressed for example in Stevens' poem, contains already its apparent opposite. You cannot have one concept of community without the other, as both Nancy and Stevens show, almost in spite of themselves.

A final peculiarity of Nancy's sentence, in its relation to the title of his book, might be expressed in two ways. 1) The terms Nancy so carefully chooses to name what has happened to community in the modern world by no means say the same thing. Each is a little strange. 2) Nancy seems to have gone out of his way to avoid using the word given worldwide currency by his friend Jacques Derrida: "deconstruction." The English translation gives *La communauté désoeuvrée* as *The Inoperative Community*, presumably because "unworked," the literal meaning of *"désoeuvrée,"* is not an ordinary English word. But "unworked," neologism or not, would much better catch the force of what Nancy wants to say in the title and in the book itself. "Inoperative" suggests a passive condition. Modern communities just do not work. They are like an inoperative piece of machinery, in need of repair. *"Désoeuvrée,"* "unworked," on the other hand, though it is used in French to describe an apparatus that is out of order, puts the stress on the process by means of which some forces or other have actively worked to dismantle community. It has not just passively happened.

"The Deconstruction of Community," in its double antithetical meaning as a simultaneous doing and undoing, constructing and taking apart, would be a good English translation of Nancy's title. Even that translation, however, would not catch the resonances of "work" in *"désoeuvrée,"* with its allusions to the Marxist or Sartrean notions of collective, communal work that has constructed communities. Marx and Sartre are important explicit references for Nancy's thinking in this book. These references embed the book in the time and place when and where it was written.

"Désoeuvrée" suggests that any human community has been constructed by collective human work. That work has put together roads, buildings, houses, machines of all kinds (including communication machines), institutions, laws, and conventions of family life to make a whole that we call a "community." Counter-work has been required in modern times to dismantle or deconstruct those material and immaterial elements of community. Having first been "worked," they now have had to be "unworked," as George W. Bush and his colleagues went far toward "unworking" or "deconstructing" the United States Constitution and the other laws and institutions that have held our national community together for over two hundred years as a fragile democracy—government of the people, by the people, and for the people.

Nancy's words, "dissolution," "dislocation," and "conflagration," are three not quite compatible terms for the unworking of community. Each implies a different model for what has happened.

"Dissolution" implies a disintegration of something once whole, as a dictator will "dissolve parliament" when he does not like the laws elected representatives are promulgating.

"Dislocation" implies that modern communities have been set outside or beside themselves, displaced. It is hard to grasp what Nancy may have had in mind when he used this word. Perhaps he meant a breaking of the ligatures that have held communities together as living, quasi-organic wholes, as when we say: "he dislocated his shoulder." The dislocation of community is the disarticulation of the bonds, the joints, which have held its members together.

"Conflagration" is the most striking word in the series. It suggests that the whole community has not only been dissolved, its parts disarticulated from one another. It has also been consumed, burned up. The more or less explicit allusion is to the Holocaust, which means of course "sacrificial burning," and to those crematoria at Auschwitz and Buchenwald. The Nazis did not simply work to make inoperative the Jewish communities within their Reich by dislocating through deportation millions of Jews, or by dissolving the family and community bonds that held together the inhabitants of the ghettos. They destroyed those communities altogether by murdering more than six million Jews in the gas chambers and then cremating their bodies, in an unspeakable conflagration.

Stevens's Model of Community

My second citation is from a poem by Wallace Stevens written in 1947. This was just the time when the Holocaust, as a turning point in Western history, was being assimilated into the American consciousness, insofar as that happened at all. "The Auroras of Autumn," as its title suggests, is a poem in which an autumnal conflagration of community is signaled by an uncanny display of northern lights.

The passage by Stevens I have cited movingly chants what it is like to live in a sequestered indigenous community. Stevens is an American poet who has expressed as well as any of our great writers a sense of homeland places, whether it is Hartford, Connecticut, where Stevens lived, or Pennsylvania Dutch country, where Stevens was born, or Florida, where he vacationed, or even Tennessee, as in "Anecdote of the Jar": "I placed a jar in Tennessee . . ." (CP, 76). One thinks of all the American place names in Stevens's poetry, for example the magical line, "The wood-doves are singing along the Perkiomen" ("Thinking of a Relation Between the Images of Metaphors," CP, 356), or of "The Idea of Order at Key West" (CP, 128-30), or of a mention of "the thin men of Haddam," in "Thirteen Ways of Looking at a Blackbird" (CP, 93), or of the line "Damariscotta da da doo" ("Variations on a Summer Day," CP, 235). "Perkiomen" is the name of a small river in Stevens's native Pennsylvania. Haddam is the name of a small town in Connecticut. Damariscotta is the name of a coastal village in Maine. It is a Native American name meaning "river of little fish." The list could be extended. Stevens's early poem "Sunday Morning" (CP, 66-70) celebrates the particularities of the United States landscape as determining the life that is lived there. Many others of Stevens' poems do the same, as in the line: "The natives of the rain are rainy men" ("The Comedian as the Letter C," CP, 37).

Just what are the salient features of an indigenous community, according to Stevens? I say "indigenous *community*" because Stevens stresses that it is an experience shared by a "we": "We were as Danes in Denmark all day long . . . ." This assumption that the indigene lives in a community of other indigenes like himself or herself is one main feature of Stevens's indigene ideology. To be an indigene is to be part of a collectivity and to have collective experience. An indigenous community, moreover, is located in a place, a milieu, an environment, an ecosystem. This milieu is cut off from the outside world, the "outlandish," the "queer," one might almost say the uncanny, in the sense implied by the German word "unheimlich," literally "unhomelike," "unhomey." Indigenes are "hale-hearted landsmen." They belong to the land, to its rocks, rivers, trees, soil, birds, fish, animals, and ways of living on the land. They would feel uprooted if they moved elsewhere. The indigene feels at home in his place, as Danes feel at home in Denmark, or as bees are at home in their honeycomb.

To be an indigene is to be innocent, childlike, almost as if asleep while awake. This innocence is like that of Adam and Eve before the fall. The indigenes know not good and evil. They do not suffer the "enigma of the guilty dream" that persecutes fallen men and women, for example the terrifying (but perhaps secretly attractive) Oedipal male dream of having killed one's father and slept with one's mother. "Enigma" refers perhaps to the Sphynx's riddle that Oedipus solved, but also to the Delphic oracle's prediction to Oedipus that he is destined to slay his father and sleep with his mother. Indigenes lack self-consciousness, as though they were sleepwalkers. They are "sticky with sleep." "Sticky" here is associated with the decorous honeycomb on which the indigenes feed. Their at-home-ness makes their milieu a kind of sleep-inducing narcotic, as eating the honey they have made puts bees to sleep. It makes them "sticky with sleep."

Not only are the indigenes not aware of themselves, with the painful self-awareness and habit of guilty introspection that is supposed to characterize Western peoples. The indigenes are also not aware of their environment, in the sense of holding it at arm's length and analyzing it. They take their milieu for granted as something that has always been there and always will be, eternally, as Denmark is for the Danes, according to Stevens. The resistance to the evidence of global warming may be generated in part by this mythical assumption that our environment is unchangeable, endlessly renewable. Why does Stevens choose Danes as exemplary of an indigenous community? I suppose because they live in a small country, have a relatively homogenous culture, and speak a "minority" language that cuts them off from others. That fits most people's idea of an indigenous community.

To mention language leads me to note that language plays a crucial role in Stevens's description. An indigenous community is created not just through shared ways of living, building, and farming on a particular homeland soil. It is also created out of language, by way of language, a particular language that belongs to that place. One radical effect of the global hegemony of Western cultural capital is to endanger, if not extinguish, so-called "minority" languages everywhere. The indigenous peoples who inhabited the State of Maine, where I live in the United States, had dwelled here for as much as twelve thousand years before the white man came. By "here" I mean right here, within a mile of where I am writing this. On a nearby shore there is a large shell midden going back at least seven thousand years. We eradicated most of the indigenes and their cultures in a couple of centuries. Only a few still speak the "native languages" of the Penobscots or the Micmacs. Their goal is often to run gambling casinos, hardly consonant with maintaining their "native culture."

To shift to the other coast, a dozen indigenous languages often disappear forever in California in a single year, as the last "native speaker" of each one of them dies. Apparently languages cannot be resuscitated when no one is left who has learned the language as a baby. Learning a language from a recording or from a grammar book does not bring a dead language back to life.

Thinking of the vanishing of indigenous languages makes the language theme in Stevens's lines all the more poignant. He sees an indigenous community as generated by language, in an act of maternal and artistic creation that mimes the creation of the world, in *Genesis*, out of the primordial darkness: "As if the innocent mother sang in the dark/Of the room and on an accordion, half-heard,/Created the time and place in which we breathed . . ./And of each other thought." Why "on an accordion"? I suppose because it is a "folk instrument." An accordion is suitable for creating the togetherness of a folk. Perhaps also it is because overtones of consonant togetherness in the word "accord" are buried in the word "accordion." The members of an indigenous community are in accord. They are "of one accord." In an assertion that recalls Heidegger's argument in *"Bauen Wohnen Denken"* ("Building Dwelling Thinking") and in his essays on Hölderlin's poems,[6] Stevens asserts that the time and place of an indigenous community are not there to begin with and then occupied by a given people. A native language creates the homeland that gives a people breathing room, a place to breathe, and therefore also a place where they can speak to one another.

Stevens's sentence just analyzed ends with the phrase, "And of each other thought." The language that creates the time and place of an indigenous community is also the medium in which the "natives" or "autochthons" think of one another. Each indigene can penetrate the minds of his or her fellows because they all speak the same language, the same "idiom," that is, a dialect peculiar to a specific group.

Indigenes speak in the "idiom of the work," that is, I take it, an idiom special to the work the innocent mother plays on the accordion. I hear also an overtone of "work" as the collective creation of an indigenous community through language and through the physical transformation of the environment. This would be akin to the Marxist notion of work or to Heidegger's notion of *"Bauen,"* building.

The mother's accordion work is also in "the idiom of an innocent earth." The earth is innocent because it too has not yet fallen with Adam and Eve's fall. The language spoken by indigenes is, as they are, born of the earth, and remains rooted in it. Language, for Stevens here, is the embodiment of thought. Each native knows what his or her fellow is thinking because, as we say, "they speak the same language." The result is that "we knew each other well," because, in Stevens's sexist formulation, "we thought alike/And that made brothers of us in a home/In which we fed on being brothers." I shall return to this exclusion of women in the invocation of "brotherhood," blood brotherhood. This at-home-ness, finally, means that the place and the community dwelling within it are sacred. These happy autochthons "lie down like children in this holiness."

Wonderful! Hooray! Or, as Stevens puts this exuberance a few lines later in "The Auroras of Autumn": "A happy people in a happy world--/ Buffo! A ball, an opera, a bar" (CP, 420). Only two problems shadow this celebration. One is that the indigenous community is a myth. It always a matter of something that hypothetically once existed and no longer exists. "We *were* as Danes in Denmark," but we no longer are. As Stevens puts this:

> There may always be a time of innocence.
> There is never a place. Or if there is no time,
> If it is not a thing of time, nor of place,
>
> Existing in the idea of it, alone,
> In the sense against calamity, it is not
> Less real. (CP, 418)

An indigenous community is real enough, but it has the reality of something that exists only in the idea of it, before time, and outside all place.

The other menace that shadows this idea is that even the mythical innocent community was always darkened by the terror of invasion. It exists as "the sense against calamity," but that calamity is always imminent. That calamity appears suddenly as a stark fear or terror just a few lines beyond the long passage I have been discussing:

Shall we be found hanging in the trees next spring?
Of what disaster is this the imminence:
Bare limbs, bare trees and a wind as sharp as salt? (CP, 419)

The poem, after all, is called "The Auroras of Autumn." Its chief figure is terrifying autumnal displays of aurora borealis or northern lights, as they presage winter and figure the conflagration of community. Simply to name all the features of an indigenous community, even in a lyric poem so celebratory of its idea as this one is, is to destroy it by bringing it self-consciously into the light. To name it is to call up its specular mirror image: the terror of its destruction. This obverse is generated out of its security, as a sense of disaster's imminence. "A happy people in a happy world" sounds, and is, too good to be true. To imagine having it is to be terrified of losing it. The imagination of being at home, in a homeland or "Heimat," instantly raises the fearful ghost of the "unheimlich," the uncanny, the terrorist at the door or probably already secretly resident somewhere inside the homeland.

Jennifer Bajorek, in a brilliant essay entitled "The Offices of Homeland Security, or, Hölderlin's Terrorism,"[7] has shown the way the rhetoric of the George W. Bush administration, in a genuinely sinister way, echoed the mystified appeal of Fascist states, for example the Nazi one. Both appeal to the notion of a "homeland" mingling *Blut und Erd*, that is, racial purity and being "rooted in one dear particular place," to borrow a phrase from Yeats.[8] Our "Department of Homeland Security" presupposes that we are a homogeneous homeland, an indigenous people whose security and racial purity are endangered by terrorists from the outside, racially and ethnically strangers, not to speak of our twelve million "illegal immigrants" or all our African-American citizens, including the present President of the United States, Barack Obama. The terrorists are probably also already inside, we are led to fear, *unheimlich* presences within the homeland. It is easy to see what is fraudulent about this use of "homeland" and "security."

I do not deny the "terrorist threat." Lots of people hate the United States and plan terrorist attacks on it. Nevertheless, the United States is not and never was a "homeland" in the sense the word implies. Relatively few United States citizens stay in the place they were born. We are nomads, even if we were born here. I was born in the state of Virginia, as were my parents and grandparents, descendents of Pennsylvania Dutch migrants into Virginia, but my family left Virginia when I was a few months old, and I have never been resident there since. The Pennsylvania Dutch were Germans (*"Deutsch"*) descended from British Hessian soldiers who surrendered during our War of Revolution. My direct ancestor on the Miller side was such a Hessian soldier. He named his son, born in 1786, "George Washington Miller," to show his patriotism, I suppose. I have lived all over the United States, as many of our citizens have. Huge numbers of our citizens, moreover, are immigrants, many quite recent immigrants, twelve million of them illegal immigrants Almost all of us are descended from immigrants who occupied an alien land. Only the tiny number of Native Americans can truly call themselves indigenes, "first people." Their ancestors too were once newcomers, travelers from Asia who crossed by the Bering land bridge just after the last ice age.

The United States is made up of an enormous diversity of different races and ethnic groups speaking many different languages. The Department of Homeland Security in its surveillance activities has made many citizens or residents of the United States markedly less secure. We are certainly far less able to maintain the privacy of our homes or of our email or of information about the books we read. Analogously, the invasion of Afghanistan and Iraq in the name of national security has arguably made our "homeland" far less secure. It has done this by multiplying many times over the terrorist threat and by leading a country like North Korea or Iran to conclude that its only possible safety lies in developing deterrent nuclear weapons as fast as possible. To be "secure," as Bajorek observes, means to be "without care." As I have shown, the myth of the indigenous community generates the terror of losing it. It generates the insecurity it would protect us against.

Bajorek's paper, in a subtle, balanced, and careful analysis, shows that Heidegger's claim that Hölderlin accepts the notions of homeland security and of an indigenous German community is a mystified misreading. Hölderlin, rather, in his poems about rivers and valleys and mountains, for example *"Heimkunft/An die Verwandten"* ("Homecoming/To the Related Ones"), read in admirable detail by Bajorek, presents the homeland as the place of lack of ground, of *"Abgrund."* The German-speaking homeland is a place of unhealed fissures and unfathomable abysses, rather than a place where an indigenous community in the sense I have identified it, with Stevens's help, could dwell. "[I]f for Hölderlin home, if and insofar as it is a place," says Bajorek, "can only be a place to which one returns, and more precisely to which one is *always* returning, this is not only because the home that man makes on this earth is not a dwelling place (*'Wohnen ist nicht das Innehaben eine Wohnung'* ['To dwell is not the occupation of a dwelling.']). It is because, for Hölderlin, 'being-there' is always a 'being-elsewhere' and first takes place by way of a departure."⁹

An Alternative Model of Community

Stevens eloquently dramatizes, but also puts in question, the ordinary commonsensical idea of human togetherness that most people have in mind, explicitly or implicitly, when they speak of community. Jean-Luc Nancy has articulated another less intuitive model of community, one inextricably entwined with the first. One resists taking Nancy's model seriously, since it is hard to think and has disastrous consequences for the first model. The second model of community "unworks" the first.

A common notion of human communities, as I have said, sees them as the construction of a group living and working together. They have made the community over time. It is the product of their combined and cooperative work, as well as the result of a social contract they have explicitly or implicitly signed. Their collective work has constituted their community, sometimes on the basis of an explicit "constitution." The communities of my university departments, if they are communities, are governed by departmental "constitutions." The community of American citizens is based on the United States Constitution, our founding document. Under George W. Bush's presidency our governance under the Constitution was deeply endangered by the executive and judiciary branches of the Federal Government.

The commonly accepted model of community sees the individuals within it as pre-existing subjectivities. These subjectivities have bound together with other subjectivities for the common good. Their mode of communication with one another can be called "intersubjectivity." This communication is an interchange between subjectivities. Such an interchange presupposes that the other is like me. Our common language makes it possible for me, in spite of my individuality, to communicate to my neighbor what I am thinking and feeling, what I am. I can, so I assume, also understand through language and other signs what the other person is thinking and feeling, what he or she is. As Stevens says, in the passage already cited, we "knew each other well, hale-hearted landsmen." These cohabiting subjectivities have made together a language, houses, roads, farms, industries, laws, institutions, religious beliefs, customs, mythical or religious stories about their origin and destiny that are told communally or written down in some sacred book to be recited to the group. Christian church services, for example, include each week readings from the Old and New Testaments that are synecdoches for a recital of the whole Bible. The entire Bible used to be read aloud in the church over the course of several years. The Bible is the sacred Book that binds a Christian community together.

Literature within such a community is the imitation, or reflection, or representation of community, the construction of cunningly verisimilar miniature models of community. *Bleak House* allows you to carry the whole of Dickens's London in your pocket. Literature is to be valued for its truth of correspondence to a community already there, for its constative value, not for any performative function it may have in constituting communities. Valid language, for example the language of literature, is primarily and fundamentally literal, not, except as embellishment, figurative, just as the conceptual terms describing this model of community are to be taken literally, *à la lettre*. The primary figure employed is the figure of synecdoche. This figure allows a few examples to stand for the whole, as Gridley, the Man from Shropshire, in *Bleak House*, stands for the whole class of those whose lives have been destroyed by the Court of Chancery.

Though the individuals living together in such a community no doubt think of themselves as mortal, and though one of their community places is the cemetery, nevertheless mortality does not essentially define community life. The community's constant renewal from generation to generation gives it a kind of collective immortality, just as the living together of individuals in a community tends to project a hypothetical sempiternal "community consciousness" or "collective consciousness." Each individual participates in, is bathed or encompassed in, this collective consciousness, as a fish swims in water, or as Danes all know Danish. Death tends to be covered over, suppressed, almost forgotten, as is notoriously the case within many American communities, if they can be called that, today.

It is possible (though it would be an error) to see Victorian novels, for example George Eliot's novels, or Charles Dickens's, or Anthony Trollope's, as straightforwardly based on such a conception of community and as reflecting or imitating actually existing communities of the sort I have been characterizing. An example of such fictive communities is the Barsetshire community in Trollope's Barset novels. The omniscient or telepathic narrators in such novels are the expression of the collective consciousness of the community I mentioned above. Victorian multi-plotted novels are, according to this view, "models of community." They are cunning miniature replicas of communities that, it is often assumed, actually existed historically. Their object of representation is not one individual life story but a whole community. The existence of such communities, in reality and in fictive simulacra, so this (false or only partially true) story about Victorian novels goes, ensures the execution of felicitous performatives. In Trollope's novels, as in Victorian fiction generally, the most important speech acts or writing acts are the marriages of young women and the passing on from generation to generation, by gifts, wills, and marriage settlements, of money, property, and rank. Most often, in Victorian novels, these two themes are combined. The heroine's marriage redistributes property, money, rank, and carries it on to the next generation.

Another model of community has been articulated in recent years. This has been done in different but more or less consonant ways by many theorists, among them those mentioned in footnote five: George Bataille, Giorgio Agamben, Alfonso Lingis, and Jean-Luc Nancy. A widely influential book by Benedict Anderson, *Imagined Communities*, is, on the whole, no more than a subtle, post-modern version of the first model of community, the one whose features I have already sketched. I shall describe the second model primarily on the basis of Nancy's *The Inoperative Community*.[10]

Nancy sees persons not as individualities but as "singularities." He sees people, that is, as agents each fundamentally different from all the others. Each singularity harbors a secret alterity that can by no means be communicated to any other singularity. These singularities are essentially marked by their finitude and by their mortality. Each is from moment to moment, from the beginning, defined by the fact that it will die. Here is Nancy's expression of this, in a passage that is cited in part by Blanchot, in *La communauté inavouable*. Blanchot says it is the fundamental affirmation in Nancy's *La communauté désoeuvrée*:

> That which is not a subject opens up onto a community whose conception, in turn, exceeds the resources of a metaphysics of the subject. Community does not weave a superior, immortal, or transmortal life between subjects (no more than it is itself woven of the inferior bonds of a consubstantiality of blood or of an association of needs), but it is constitutively, to the extent that it is a matter of a "constitution" here, calibrated on the death of those whom we call, perhaps wrongly, its "members" (inasmuch as it is not a question of an organism). But it does not make a work of this calibration. Community no more makes a work out of death than it is itself a work. The death upon which community is calibrated does not *operate* the dead being's passage into some communal intimacy, nor does community, for its part, *operate* the transfiguration of its dead into some substance or subject—be these homeland, native soil or blood, nation, a delivered or fulfilled humanity, absolute phalanstery [This word means "a community of the followers of Charles Fourier," from *phalanx* ("any close-knit or compact body of people") plus *monastère*, monastery.], family, or mystical body. Community is calibrated on death as on that of which it is precisely impossible to *make a work* (other than a work of death, as soon as one tries to make a work of it). Community occurs in order to acknowledge this impossibility, or more exactly—for there is neither function nor finality here—the impossibility of making a work out of death is inscribed and acknowledged as "community."

Community is revealed in the death of others; hence it is always revealed to others. Community is what takes place always through others and for others. It is not the space of the *egos*—subjects and substances that are at bottom immortal—but of the I's, who are always *others* (or else are nothing). If community is revealed in the death of others, it is because death itself is the true community of I's that are not *egos*. It is not a communion that fuses the *egos* into an *Ego* or a higher *We*. It is the community of *others*. The genuine community of mortal beings, or death as community, establishes their impossible communion. Community therefore occupiers a singular place: it assumes the impossibility of its own immanence, the impossibility of a communitarian being in the form of a subject. In a certain sense community acknowledges and inscribes—this is its peculiar gesture—the impossibility of community. (IC, 14-15).

The reader will see that Nancy's model of community puts in question, point by point, all the features of Stevens's indigenous community, the community of those who live together like Danes in Denmark. Each singularity, in Nancy's model of community, is not a self-enclosed subjectivity, such as the first model assumes. Each singularity is exposed, at its limit, to a limitless or abyssal outside that it shares with the other singularities, from the beginning, by way of their common mortality. Their community is defined by the imminence of death. This death we experience not in our own deaths, since they cannot be "experienced," but in the death of another, the death of our friend, our neighbor, our relative. The language defining this other model of community is, necessarily, figurative, catachrestic, since no literal language exists for it. Even conceptual words are used "anasemically" by Nancy, that is, against the grain of their dictionary meanings. They are also used with an implicit or explicit play on their metaphorical roots. Examples of such words in Nancy's book are "*singularité*" itself, or "*désoeuvrée*," or "*partagé*," or "*com-parution*," or "*limite*," or "*exposition*," or "*interruption*," or even "*littérature*," as in Nancy's phrase "literary communism." Blanchot's complex use of the word "*désastre*" in *L'écriture du désastre*, is another example. I give the words in the original French, because their nuances are not easily translated.

The first model of community is easy to understand because it is the one most of "us" take for granted. Nancy's model is more difficult to understand or to think. Moreover, as I have said, one resists thinking it or taking it seriously because it is devastating, a disaster, for the other model. Nancy's systematic dismantling of that other model's assumptions confirms that. No subjectivities, no intersubjective communication, no social "bonds," no collective consciousness, exist in Nancy's "unworked community." This set of negations is perhaps what leads Jacques Derrida to say of Nancy's theory of community: "Why call it a community? Just to conform to what certain of our friends have attempted to do, to Blanchot's 'unavowable' community or Nancy's 'inoperative' [*désoeuvrée*] one? I have no qualms about these communities; my only question is, why call them communities?"[11]

Nancy carries on his thinking about community by permutation of certain recurrent key terms. These words are incorporated again and again in new formulations. These attempt once more to say what cannot be said. They keep trying to say what is, strictly speaking, unsayable. The last sentence of *The Inoperative Community* in the original French form, avers just this. (The original version has just the first three chapters of the five chapters in the English version.) "Here I must interrupt myself: it is up to you to allow to be said what no one, no subject, can say, and what exposes us in common" (IC, 81).

This essential "impossibility of saying" determines several features of Nancy's style. First, the key words he uses are twisted away from their normal or casual use. They are suspended from everyday discourse. They are, as it were, held out in the open, dangling, unattached, since they tend to detach themselves through their iteration in different syntactic combinations with other key words. The reader notices them as separate, somewhat enigmatic, locutions. A second stylistic feature is outright contradiction, unsaying in the same sentence what has just been said, as in "allow to be said what no one, no subject, can say." Well, if no subject can say it, who or what can be imagined to say it? A third feature is an odd sort of implicit spatialization of the story Nancy tells. The figures of limit, sharing/shearing (*"partage"*), articulation, suspension, exposition, and so on, are all implicitly spatial. These words invite the reader to think again what Nancy is thinking in terms of a certain weird space, in which the topographical terms are withdrawn as soon as they are proffered. The limit, for example, is not an edge, border, or frontier, since there is nothing that can be confronted beyond it. It is like the cosmologists' finite but unbounded universe. You confront a limit, a boundary, but you cannot get out of your enclosure because no beyond exists, no transcendent outside. "*Partagé*," to give another example, is a double antithetical word meaning both shared and sheared. It is a spatial or topographical word, but you cannot easily map something that is both shared and sheared, "*partagé*." Nancy has written a whole book, *Le Partage des voix*,[12] exploiting the contradictory nuances of the French word "*partage*."

A final feature of Nancy's style (which is to say, of his "thought") is that the model of community he proposes is explicitly the negation (though that is not quite the right word) of the community model that most people have in mind when one asks, "What is a community?" The two models are not antithetical or negations of one another, in the Hegelian sense of a determinate negation allowing for dialectical sublation. Each presupposes the other, is entangled with the other, is generated by the other as soon as you try to express it alone, for example in a novel or in a theoretical treatise, such as Nancy's or such as these paragraphs you are now reading, or such as the lines from Stevens I read earlier. The "ideological" model presupposes pre-existing self-enclosed "individuals," "subjectivities," "selves," "persons." These egos are finite no doubt, mortal no doubt, but totalizing, oriented toward totality, and in that sense immortal. These individuals then encounter other individuals and subsequently establish, by intersubjective communication leading to a compact or contract, a society, a community made up of shared stories (myths of origin and end), a language, institutions, laws, customs, family structures with rules for marriage and inheritance, gender roles and so on, all organically composed and all the combined work of individuals living together. A group of people living and working together establishes an immanent close-knit community, geographically located, closed in on itself, autochthonous, indigenous. Language is a tool that "works," or makes, or produces, the interchanges of community.

Nancy says we now know no such community ever existed, though the first sentence of *The Inoperative Community* reaffirms this familiar historical myth. This myth or ideologeme presumes such communities once existed and that modernity is characterized by their dissolution: "The gravest and most painful testimony of the modern world," says Nancy in the passage already cited in the introduction, " the one that possibly gathers together all other testimonies which this epoch finds itself charged with assuming, by virtue of who knows what decree or necessity (for we bear witness also to the exhaustion of thinking by way of History), is the testimony of the dissolution, the dislocation, or the conflagration of community" (IC, 1). The commonly presumed model is always already unworked, *désoeuvré*, by the alternative model. That model is a negation, if not in the dialectical sense allowing some synthesizing "*aufhebung*," or sublation, then at least in the sense that it says no to the other one. It defines itself point by point as opposed to the "first" model. In place of individuals with self-enclosed subjectivities, Nancy puts singularities that are aboriginally "*partagés*," shared, sheared, open to an abyssal outside called death, sharing in it willynilly. Singularities are extroverted, exposed to other singularities at the limit point where everything vanishes. Language in such a community becomes literature, "writing" in the Blanchotian or Derridean sense, not sacred myth. Literature becomes the enactment of the performative unworking of community.

Here is a key example of Nancy's mode of expressing both what the "unworked" or "inoperative" community is like, and also the way it differs from traditional notions of social bonds and of intersubjective communication. A long citation is necessary. The passage is by no means all that easy to understand. I give it in the English translation, though with French words or phrases along the way where the nuance of the French is important:

> Communication consists before all else in this sharing and in this compearance (*com-parution*) of finitude: that is, in the dislocation and in the interpellation that reveal themselves to be constitutive of being-in-common—precisely inasmuch as being-in-common is not a common being. The finite-being exists first of all according to a division of sites, according to an extension—*partes extra partes*—such that each singularity is extended (in the sense that Freud says: "The psyche is extended"). It is not enclosed in a form—although its whole being touches against its singular limit—but it is what it is, singular being (singularity of being), only through its extension, through the areality that above all extroverts it in its very being—whatever the degree or the desire of its "egoism"—and that makes it exist only *by exposing it to an outside*.

This outside is in its turn nothing other than the exposition of another areality, of another singularity—the same other. This exposure, or this exposition-sharing, gives rise, from the outset, to a mutual interpellation of singularities prior to any address in language (though it gives to this latter its first condition of possibility). Finitude compears, that is to say it is exposed: such is the essence of community.

Under these conditions, communication is not a bond. The metaphor of the "social bond" unhappily superimposes upon "subjects" (that is to say, objects) a hypothetical reality (that of the "bond") upon which some have attempted to confer a dubious "intersubjective" nature that would have the virtue of attaching these objects to one another. This would be the economic link or the bond of recognition. But compearance is of a more originary order than that of the bond. It does not set itself up, it does not establish itself, it does not emerge among already given subjects (objects). It consists of the appearance of the *between* as such: you *and* I (between us)—a formula in which the *and* does not imply juxtaposition, but exposition. What is expressed in compearance is the following, and we must learn to read it in all its possible combinations: "you (are/and/is) (entirely other than) I" ("*toi [e(s)t] [tout autre que] moi*"). Or again, more simply, "*you shares me*" ("*toi partage moi*").

Only in this communication are singular beings given—without a bond *and* without communion, equally distant from any notion of connection or joining from the outside and from any notion of a common or fusional interiority. Communication is the constitutive fact of an exposition to the outside that defines singularity. In its being, in its very being, singularity is exposed to the outside. By virtue of this position or this primordial structure, it is at once detached, distinguished, and communitarian. Community is the presentation of the detachment (or retrenchment) of this distinction that is not individuation, but finitude compearing. (IC, 29)

"Compearing," as I said at the outset of this chapter, means "appearing together," a variant of "appearance." "*Comparution,*" in French, means "an action of *comparaître*." "*Comparaître*" means presenting oneself by order, for example the order of a court, so the judge can adjudicate between conflicting accounts. The assumption that being with, or "finitude compearing," is a fundamental feature of human existence is the basic presupposition of Nancy's other big book about community, *Being Singular Plural*.[13] Nancy argues tirelessly in this book that the "with" of "being with" goes all the way to the bottom, so to speak, both of each individual ego and of Being in general. We cannot help but share our existence with others. For Nancy, "being" is always already simultaneously divided and unified by the togetherness of a plural being-with. We are each both singular and plural at once, as in Nancy's punning title, "Being Singular Plural," where "Being" ("*Être*") is both a noun and a verb. Here is one example of Nancy's way of expressing this complex assumption:

> That Being is being-with, absolutely, this is what we must think. The *with* is the most basic feature of Being, the mark [*trait*] of the singular plurality of the origin or origins in it. . . . What is proper to community, then, is given to us in the following way: it has no other resource to appropriate except the "with" that constitutes it, the *cum* of "community," its interiority without an interior, and nevertheless perhaps it too, after its fashion, *interior intimo suo* [(has) its own intimate interior]. As a result, this *cum* is the *cum* of co-appearance, wherein we do nothing but appear together with one another, co-appearing before no other authority [*l'instance*] than this "with" itself, the meaning of which seems to us instantly to dissolve into insignificance, into exteriority, into the inorganic, empirical, and randomly contingent [*aléatoire*] inconsistency of the pure and simple "with." (BSP, 61-2, 63, trans. altered; ESP, 83-4, 85)

If "myth," for Nancy, is the linguistic expression of those living together according to the first model of community, "literature" names the contestation of that by one expression or another, however implicit, of the second model of community. This gives literature (which includes, for Nancy, philosophy, theory, and criticism, as well as literature proper in the sense of novels, poems, and plays) an explicitly political function, as he asserts at the end of "Le communisme littéraire," the third and final part of *La communauté désoeuvrée* in its original French version:

> It is because there is community—unworked (*désoeuvrée*) always, and resisting at the heart of every collectivity and in the heart of every individual—and because myth is interrupted—suspended always, and divided by its own enunciation—that there exists the exigency of "literary communism." And this means: thinking, the practice of a sharing of voices (*un partage des voix*) and of an articulation according to which there is no singularity but that exposed in common, and no community but that offered to the limit of singularities.
>
> This does not determine any particular mode of sociality, and it does not found a politics—if a politics can ever be "founded." But it defines at least a limit, at which all politics stop and begin. The communication that takes place on this limit, and that, in truth, constitutes it, demands that way of destining ourselves in common that we call a politics, that way of opening community to itself, rather than to a destiny or to a future. "Literary communism" indicates at least the following: that community, in its infinite resistance to everything that would bring it to completion (in every sense of the word "*achever*"—which can also mean "finish off"), signifies an irrepressible political exigency, and that this exigency in its turn demands something of "literature," the inscription of our infinite resistance.
>
> It defines neither *a* politics, nor <u>a</u> writing, for it refers, on the contrary, to that which resists any definition or program, be these political, aesthetic, or philosophical. But it cannot be accommodated within every "politics" or within every "writing." It signals a bias in favor of the "literary communist" resistance that precedes us rather than our inventing it—that precedes us from the depths of community. A politics that does not want to know anything about this is a mythology, or an

economy. A literature that does not say anything about it is a mere diversion, or a lie. (IC, 80-1; CD, 197-8)

The reader will see that Nancy's model of an inoperative community is based on a strange contradictory spatial model in which singularities are at one and the same time enclosed within unbreachable "limits" and at the same time exposed, across or through those limits, to all the other singularities, in a pre-originary "with" or "being with." This being with is always already there, as a fundamental feature of every singularity, but it is also an infinite abyss, the place where each singularity joins all the others.

One more question must be asked and an answer posited. If the first kind of community ensures the felicitous uttering of performatives—promises, marriage oaths, contracts, wills, and the like—what about speech acts in the second kind of community? No solid ground for doing things with words is offered by the community joining a "set, a group of 'exposed' singularities that are wholly other to one another." This joining takes place by way of the impossibility of community. None of the conditions for felicitous speech acts laid out by Austin in *How to Do Things with Words* is met within an "unworked community." The members are not enclosed selves or egos capable of taking responsibility for what they say and enduring through time so that promises made yesterday may be kept today. No social contract or constitution making possible the establishment of functioning laws and institutions exists. No transparent "intersubjective" communication, no social bond, can be counted on to certify for me the sincerity of speech acts uttered by another person.

Such a community is *"inavouable,"* unavowable, in the double sense that Blanchot means the word in *La communauté inavouable* (*The Unavowable Community*). An unworked community remains secret, unable to be publicly avowed. Blanchot's example is the secret community Georges Bataille and his associates established. This was a community committed to the clandestine sacrifice of one or another of its members by beheading (hence the name *"Acéphale"*). Such a community is certainly something one would want to keep secret, though one might note that the early secret communities of Christians performed a ritual sacrifice, commemorating Christ's crucifixion, in the communion service. This ceremony was modeled on the sacrifices, sometimes actually bloody, in ancient Near Eastern mystery cults. United States solidarity is held together today, it might be argued, by the sacrificial enactment, over and over again, of the "death penality."

Such an unworked community is "unavowable" in another way, however. It does not provide solid ground for any avowals or speech acts. This does not mean that speech acts do not occur within unworked communities, nor that they may not be efficacious. What it does mean, however, is that such speech acts are not endorsed by any public laws and institutions. They work by a resolution to go on being true to them that is continuously self-generated and self-sustained. Such speech acts are kind of lifting oneself by one's own bootstraps over that abyss to which Nancy and Blanchot give the name "death."

Matthew Arnold expresses something like this form of unavowable vow in the contradictory last stanza of "Dover Beach." Arnold's formulation is Blanchotian in its positing of a love between singularities that is without grounds in love as a universal, Love with a capital L. Nor does it have grounds in any of the other universals, certitude, peace, joy, light, and so on, that would seem necessary prerequisites for felicitous vows of fidelity exchanged between lovers. Arnold's speaker exhorts his beloved to join him in what Blanchot might have called an *"amour sans amour."* This would be the only love possible in an unworked community:

> Ah, love, let us be true
> To one another! for the world, which seems
> To lie before us like a land of dreams,
> So various, so beautiful, so new,
> Hath really neither joy, nor love, nor light,
> Nor certitude, nor peace, nor help for pain...[14]

One word cognate with "community," "communion," leads Nancy's reflection to remarks on Christian communion and on Freud's theories of the primal horde. Here a challenge to Nancy by Jacques Derrida will help me to refine further the two notions of community I am juxtaposing. Derrida's target is not Nancy's *La communauté désoeuvré* but his *L'experience de la liberté*. The members of a community of the first kind are in communion with one another by way of what they share. What they share, according to Freud, is that the have killed the father and have shared/sheared his body and eaten it. This makes them "brothers" and "*semblables*." Baudelaire hails the "*hypocrite lecteur* (hypocritical reader)" of *Fleurs du mal* as "*mon semblable, -- mon frère*."[15] All the members of the primal horde are the same. They share a guilt, the murder of the father. They are all like one another, hence transparent to one another, like the brothers in Stevens's poem. The culture of Stevens's brothers, you will remember, is generated by the mother's song on the accordion. The French revolutionary motto, "liberty, equality, fraternity," links freedom to fraternity. That freedom needed to be asserted in a violent act against monarchal sovereignty. The French revolutionaries shared the guilt of killing the king. Modern English democracy has the beheading of King Charles on its conscience. The Alhambra in Granada, Spain, was the scene of the killing of the primal father in reverse. The Sultan had thirty-six princes, his sons, beheaded. The Fountain of the Lions ran with their blood.

A fraternal community is united in its opposition to those who are not *semblables*, who are different, who do not take communion, who do not repeat Christ's words to his disciples, a brotherhood if there ever was one: "This do in remembrance of me." Such a community is a community of intolerance, often of unspeakable cruelty to those outside the community, as the Christians expelled Arabs and Jews from Spain. Such a community depends for its solidarity on exclusion. You are either with us or against us, and if you are against us you are "evil-doers," as George W. Bush called Iraq, North Korea, Somali, etc., in the end every other nation but the United States, and then only a small group there, the rest being sympathizers, "focus groups," peaceniks, communists, subversives, friends of terrorism, in short, evil-doers. This happens by an implacable and frightening suicidal logic that is built into democracy defined as a brotherhood of *semblables*. Ultimately only Bush and his cronies would be left, and then they would begin bumping one another off. This did indeed happen, as one or another of them "fell on his sword" by resigning and disappearing from public view, even while Bush still ruled. Where is Donald Rumsfeld now? Or John Ashcroft? The Teapartyers today (2010) are held together, if you can call it that, by the same perverse logic.

Where are the women in this paradigm, the sisters, mothers, wives, lovers? Are they *semblables*? Maurice Blanchot thinks they are rather members of a different sort of community, as did Marguerite Duras. In "The Community of Lovers," in *The Unavowable Community*, Blanchot proposes, on the basis of a reading of Marguerite Duras's récit, *The Malady of Death*, and with reference to Emmanuel Levinas and to the story of Tristan and Isolde, another version of the "unavowable community" he has delineated in the first part of his book. This one is the impossible "community of two" made up of lovers:

> And let us also remember that even the reciprocity of the love relationship, as Tristan and Isolde's story represents it, the paradigm of shared love, excludes simple mutuality as well as a unity where the Other would blend with the same. And this brings us back to the foreboding that passion eludes possibility, eluding, for those caught by it, their own powers, their own decision and even their "desire," in that it is strangeness itself, having consideration neither for what they can do nor for what they want, but luring them into a strangeness where they become estranged from themselves, into an intimacy which also estranges them from each other. And thus, eternally separated, as if death was in them, between them? Not separated, not divided: inaccessible and, in the inaccessible, in an infinite relationship.[16]

Jacques Derrida, in *Voyous*, is closer to Blanchot than to Nancy's notion of a brotherhood of free men. Against Nancy, and with a covert allusion to Levinas, Derrida poses a (non)community of dissimilars, of non-semblables. This (non)community is made up of neighbors who are defined by their absolute difference from on another: ". . . pure ethics, if there is any, begins with the respectable dignity of the other as the absolute *unlike* (*à la dignité respectable de l'autre comme absolu* dissemblable*)*, recognized as nonrecognizable, indeed as unrecognizable (*reconnu comme non reconnaissable, voire comme méconnaissable*) beyond all knowledge, all cognition and all recognition: far from being the beginning of pure ethics, the neighbor as like or as resembling, as looking like (*comme semblable ou resssemblant*), spells the end or the ruin of such an ethics, if there is any."[17]

Derrida is even more explicit in his disagreement with Nancy in a forceful passage in his last, as yet unpublished, seminars, and in a direct reference to Nancy's theory of community in one of the interviews in *A Taste for the Secret*, already cited. "Why call it a community?" asks Derrida in the interview. In the seminar Derrida says, in his most intransigent expression of his sense that each "I" is isolated, enisled like Robinson Crusoe before he encountered Friday:

> Between my world, the "my world," what I call "my world," and there is no other for me, every other world making up part of it, between my world and every other world, there is initially the space and the time of an infinite difference, of an interruption incommensurable with all the attempts at passage, of bridge, of isthmus, of communication, of translation, of trope, and of transfer that the desire for a world and the sickness of the world [*mal du monde*], the being in sickness of the world [*l'être en mal de monde*] will attempt to pose, to impose, to propose, to stabilize. There is no world, there are only islands.[18]

Suppose one were to take seriously Nancy's notion of a community of singularities, or, in Lingis's phrase, a community of those who have nothing in common. How would this lead one to think differently from the way Fengzhen Wang and Shabao Xie do in a recent essay the effects of globalization? Wang and Xie argue that globalization is destroying local cultures everywhere, transforming indigenes into cybersurfers.[19] One might respond that Wang and Xie are using Western concepts of local communities. Nancy's conception of community and the tradition to which it belongs, as well as Wallace Stevens's contrary model, are both as much Western inventions as are any other products of cultural capitalism, as is Derrida's repudiation of togetherness as something primordially given. Nancy's community of singularities is Western through and through. Nevertheless, it is, like other such products, asserted by Nancy with apodictic universality. It is not just Western men and women who are singularities exposed to others at the limit, according to him, but all men and women everywhere at all times. Nevertheless, Nancy's ideas are a Western product, perhaps even a product of the resources of the French language. I do not see any way out of this aporia. Any idea of community will be idiomatic, the product of a given language, but will tend to express itself as universal. Nevertheless, it would be plausible to argue that each community should have its own singular idea of community, appropriate only for that community alone. In that case, the whole issue of *Ariel* devoted to thinking in English about globalization and about the destruction of indigenous cultures would be a form of the thing it would resist.

The second thing to say if we take Nancy's model of community seriously, is that it disqualifies, to some degree at least, Wang and Xie's opposition between the happy indigene and the cybersurfer, penetrated through and through by global capitalism, corrupted by it, deprived of his or her specificity and made the same as everyone else. Wang and Xie put it this way: "Multinational capital with its hegemonic ideology and technology seems to be globally erasing difference, imposing sameness and standardization on consciousness, feeling, imagination, motivation, desire, and taste."[20] According to Nancy's model of community, the singularity of neither indigene nor cybersurfer is touched by the interpellations of indigeneous culture, for the former, and leveling American popular culture, for the other. Beneath these superficial cultural garments both indigene and cybersurfer remain singular, wholly other to one another, though exposed to the others, even though they may be either living together as indigenes or, on the contrary, communicating, via email, online chats, texting, or "tweets," as cybersurfers. To put this in Heideggerian terms, the loneliness of *Dasein*, fundamentally characterized by its "*Sein zum Tode*" ("Being towards death"), remains intact beneath the alienating superficialities of *das Man*, the "they," and even beneath the most dramatic technological, political, and social changes. It is as true as ever now that each man or woman dies his or her own death.

Nevertheless, it is plausible to argue that dwelling within the uniqueness of a so-called indigenous culture, that is, a local way of living untouched by globalization, if such a thing anywhere remains these days, is a better way to live the otherness of singularities in their exposure to one another than the global homogenizing culture that is rapidly becoming the most widely experienced way to be human today. Diversity of cultures, languages, idioms, it can be argued, is a good in itself, just as is a diversity of plant and animal species. Moreover, certain local cultures, it may be, are closer to recognizing the imminence of death in their religious and cultural expressions than is Western popular culture's bland avoidance of death through its banal spectacular presentation of death in cinema and television. Global capitalism has to be resisted by each local culture as best it can. One way, as Nancy suggests, is through what he calls "communist literature," that is, literature, including philosophy and critical theory, as well as poems, novels, cinema, and television shows, that does not avoid confrontation with singularity, even though it cannot be confronted. Blanchot's "*récits*" might be models of such literature. Perhaps little of that kind of literature exists any longer, though Kafka, Kertész, and Morrison are examples of its persistence, as my readings will attempt to show.

The leveling effects of global cultural capitalism are enormously powerful, but small-scale local ways exist to resist those forces in the name of the idiomatic and the singular. Though Western critical theory and literature are concomitants of global cultural capitalism, they can be used to support resistance to global leveling, just as the telecommunications products of capitalism can be mobilized against some aspects of it, as in the use of the Internet in Barack Obama's campaign for president in the United States in the summer and fall of 2008. It is a matter of strategic deployment, not necessarily of passive submission to an inevitable Juggernaut. Or rather, the resistance to global capitalism is a matter of certain anomalous speech acts performed within "indigenous communities" now seen as gatherings of singularities. These speech acts perform local transformations of the global situation that might just possibly help maintain local communities of singularities. Somewhat paradoxically, another Western product, its secular literary writings, for instance Wallace Stevens's poems or Victorian novels, or the novels discussed in this book, often assert the unknowable singularity of fictive or poetic personae, for example in the crucial decisions they are shown making. Demonstrating that persuasively for some novels written before and after Auschwitz by Franz Kafka, Imre Kertész, Toni Morrison, and others, is one goal of this book.

I do not think much is gained by vilifying new telecommunication technologies as a cause of the conflagration of community. Cinema, television, cell phones, computers, and the Internet are, as media, to some degree neutral, in spite of the way their existence radically transforms any "indigenous" culture that begins to use them. In spite of the differences between Network TV and Cable TV, versions of the same Television technology are used to broadcast the PBS News Hour and to broadcast Fox so-called "News." The Internet stores and distributes with indifference and equanimity both the rantings of Holocaust deniers and horrible photographs of a *Selektion* at Auschwitz. Even so, the media that transmit these "contents" change what is formatted for transmission. Blogging technology is indifferent to what is posted on the blogs. The cultural force of these devices depends on the uses that are made of them, even though they have in themselves, as media, enormous force in transforming the ways we think and feel, along with our relations to others, as I have argued in *The Medium Is the Maker*.[21]

New telecommunication devices, for example the iPhone, can be used to reinforce and preserve local languages and local ways of life, however difficult it may be to do that. An essay several years ago in *Scientific American*, "Demystifying the Digital Divide,"[22] distinguished sharply between projects that simply set up computers in "underdeveloped countries," in which case they are likely to be used primarily to play computer games, thereby destroying the local culture, and those projects, like one in an impoverished region of southern India, that use computer installations to help support and maintain an indigenous culture. I would add that the new medium, nevertheless, transforms any culture that uses it, as print book culture transformed medieval manuscript culture in the West. In the few years since that *Scientific American* article was published, computers, cell phones, iPhones, iPods, and Blackberries have become far more widely distributed around the world than they were in 2003, just as the distinction between "developed" and "underdeveloped" countries is fading. One sees as many people using cell phones on the streets of Beijing as in New York or Frankfurt. An enormous recent scholarly literature, following pioneer work by Katherine Hayles, Donna Harroway, and Derrida, analyzes the nature and effects of new digital media in their "intermediation" with print media.[23] The consensus is that an extremely rapid "critical climate change" is occurring by way of new media that is effecting even what it means to be human or "post-human." Some of this work pays attention to the question of what one might mean by an online "community," a computer game-playing community, or a Facebook or Twitter community, that is, communities generated by new teletechnologies. That, however, is a question for another book.

Nevertheless, it important to remember that it is a fundamental feature of our present-day relation to the Shoah that it is mediated to such a large degree by new digital communication technologies, for example online photographs of a *Selektion* or Wikipedia entries on "Auschwitz" or "Buchenwald." The Shoah was made possible by the technologies, including communication technologies, of its day. Much of what we know and feel now about the Shoah comes by way of our current teletechnologies: films like Claude Lanzmann's *Shoah*, surviving photographs, and electronic recordings of testimony by survivors. Art Spiegelman's *Maus* is available on a DVD, as is the film of Kertész's *Fatelessness*, Such artifactualities, it may be, generate communities of survivors of the survivors, though, as my chapter on Kertész, will argue, by way of another essay by Jean-Luc Nancy, "Forbidden Representation," representing the Shoah in any medium is extremely problematic. Even a visit, for example, to Buchenwald, such as I made in November, 2009, with an extremely knowledgeable guide for our group, does not tell you much. Buchenwald is now so clean, so neat, so sweetsmelling, even the surviving crematorium. It is now almost, but not quite, a tourist attraction, even though horrors took place there on a grand scale. The visitor can come and go as he or she pleases, which was not the case for the hundreds of thousands imprisoned there, many of whom died in the camp.

A Third Paradigm for Communities

I turn now, in concluding this chapter, to a brief account of another model of community, or rather of communities. This other model exists in several forms. It is, moreover, exemplified, as I shall suggest in later chapters, in different ways by the novels read in this book. I have spoken so far, following both Stevens and Nancy, as if a community of any kind must be thought of as a sequestered group of people all related or, perhaps, non-related to one another in various ways. This third model thinks of a given society as made rather of a group of overlapping and interrelated communities, no one of which exists in total isolation from the others.

One should, if following this paradigm, always speak of "communities" not of a "community." Any modern social group, such as a nation, this model would claim, is made up of a large number of interwoven institutions, bureaucracies, agencies, and what Foucault calls "*dispositifs*" ("apparatuses"). For Foucault, "*dispositif*" is a name for the machine-like working of the whole social-legal-governmental-financial-bureaucratic assemblage in a given society at a given time. A willing worker for such an apparatus is called, in Sovietese, an "apparatchik." This apparatus, said Foucault, is "a thoroughly heterogeneous set consisting of discourses, institutions, architectural forms, regulatory decisions, laws, administrative measures, scientific statements, philosophical, moral, and philanthropic propositions—in short, the said as much as the unsaid. Such are the elements of the apparatus."[24] Kafka's "office writings," the bureaucratic documents he produced as a high-ranking lawyer in Prague in the largest Workman's Accident Insurance Institute in the Czech Lands of the Austro-Hungarian Empire are a splendid example of such "discourses."[25] The concepts of heterogeneity, of lateral as well as vertical proliferation, and of the machinal, as opposed to the organic, are essential to mappings of this third model of communities.

Today Foucault might have added to his litany of wielders of power the media, including the Internet. Each element in the heterogeneous assemblage he calls an "apparatus" is determined by the use it makes of the information technologies available at a given time. Sociologists have studied the dependence of old-fashioned bureacracies on offices crammed with paper that secretaries type or write and that are circulated from office to office, up, down, and transversely among the proliferating hierarchies. Kafka's novels especially dramatize such bureaucracies, though the other novels I read in this book also exemplify them. The Holocaust was perpetrated by means of efficient ramifying German governmental bureaucracies with the cooperation of bureaucracies, including police bureaucracies, within conquered countries like Hungary. The complex interrelation of these agencies was calculated to make it difficult for the left hand to know what the right hand was doing, or writing. Slavery in the United States, my topic in Part Four of this book, was also generated and controlled by a complex apparatus of interconnected institutions, businesses, laws, and customs. This went from the purchase by slave traders of captured Africans in Africa to their transportation in the slave trade by way of the notorious "Middle Passage," to their resale in the United States, to their frequent reselling at auction in the United States, to the regulations and customs governing (sometimes) their treatment on plantations, to the slaves' establishment of fragile families, churches, and communities on the plantations, to such pre-Civil War legal institutions as the Fugitive Slave Law, to their emancipation followed by the subsequent century of southern Jim Crow laws, segregation, widespread lynchings, and so on. Slavery would have been impossible without this complicated legal, social, and commercial apparatus, all using the media of the day, such as posters to advertise slave auctions or the widespread circulation in the south of postcards with photographs of lynchings.

To turn to the present day: the recent collapse of the global financial system has depended on immensely complex use of computers and the Internet. Louis Althusser includes the media among ISAs, Ideological State Apparatuses, in his famous essay on ideology's interpellations.[26] It is a distinguishing feature, as I have said, of a given example of such an all-embracing social apparatus that it operates on its own, robot-like. What it brings about is "Nobody's Fault," to cite the title Dickens first presciently intended for *Little Dorrit*, with its Kafka-like presentation of the English Circumlocution Office. The latter is the model of an efficient bureaucracy of many layers receding to invisibility that just goes on and on, like the Energizer bunny, doing its intended work of procrastination. This is parallel to the legal system in Kafka's *Der Prozeß* (*The Trial*), or, in a different form, to the bureaucracy binding the village to the castle, while at the same time separating them, in Kafka's *Das Schloß* (*The Castle*).

Three other modes of this alternative paradigm, each substantially different from the others, may be briefly described, to bring this preliminary chapter to an end. Each would merit a lengthy exposition.

Stanley Fish's idea of "interpretive communities," as developed especially in *Is There a Text in This Class?*,[27] presupposes that the university and those societies within which universities operate are made up of distinct groups of people who take certain interpretive assumptions for granted as objective and universal, though the groups are incompatible with one another, and though no solid foundation for such assumptions exists. One group reads, for example, Milton's poems in one way, while another interpretive community reads Milton quite differently, though both assume, incorrectly, that the Milton they see is *there*, objectively. Similarly, teapartyers and progressive democrats today interpret our present situation in the United States in strikingly opposed ways, though to each it seems that their ideological vision is objective truth.

I have already referred to Derrida's putting in question of Nancy's idea of the inoperative community. Derrida tends rather to think of each person's possible participation in a multitude of partially overlapping communities or institutions, as in the humanities communities in the university he addresses in *L'université sans condition* (*The University without Condition*).[28] In a striking passage in *A Taste for the Secret*, a passage that I have discussed in more detail in the chapter "Derrida Enisled," in my *For Derrida*,[29] Derrida affirms his unwillingness to belong to any of these intermeshed communities. "I am not one of the family," says Derrida, echoing André Gide. He then goes on to list the various communities to which he refuses to belong. Derrida's sees society as a complex structure made up of multiple proliferating communities, side by side, overlapping, or one inside others:

> …let me get back to my saying "I am not one of the family." Clearly, I was playing on a formula that has multiple registers of resonance. I'm not one of the family means, in general, "I do not define myself on the basis of my belonging to the family," or to civil society, or to the state; I do not define myself on the basis of elementary forms of kinship. But it also means, more figuratively, that I am not part of any group, that I do not identify myself with a linguistic community, a national community, a political party, or with any group or clique whatsoever, with any philosophical or literary school. "I am not one of the family" means: do not consider me "one of you," "don't count me in," I want to keep my freedom, always: this, for me, is the condition not only for being singular and other, but also for entering into relation with the singularity and alterity of others. When someone is one of the family, not only does he lose himself in the herd [*gregge*, in the Italian version], but he loses the others as well; the others become simply places, family functions, or places or functions in the organic totality

that constitutes a group, school, nation, or community of subjects speaking the same language.³⁰

Derrida experiences himself as being besieged on all sides by exhortations, interpellations, calls, demands, addresses, beseechings, invocations, convocations, hailings, that he say "Yes!" and accept his belonging to this or that one of the superimposed communities large and small with which he is surrounded. He must say a resolute "No!" to all if he is to maintain his own integrity along with the possibility of genuine ethical relations to others. It is the most extreme and intransigent refusal of community I know. Nevertheless, Derrida was, whatever he said about refusing to belong, in himself the center of a complex global set of interlocking communities. He had manifold belongings to institutions and groups all over the world, to the universities that hired him to teach or to lecture, to a network of translators and publishing houses, to archives, to sponsors of colloquiums and conferences on his work, to film-makers, to friends.

My final example of the model of overlapping heterogeneous communities is Deleuze and Guattari's concept of the social and linguistic rhizome. It is worked out in the most detail in "Introduction: Rhizome" at the beginning of *A Thousand Plateaus*.³¹ Though Deleuze and Guattari's model is complex, subtle, and, as is usual with them, exuberantly creative, the bottom line is a rejection of any subject/object paradigm and a resistance either to a unitary model like Stevens's and Nancy's, or to a hierarchical concept modeled on a tree's root, trunk, and dividing branches, as in a genealogical tree or as in the genetic tree that anthropologists use to trace our ancestry back to the apes. In place of those, Deleuze and Guattari put as mapping the rhizomatic plant that proliferates laterally, producing new plants growing up from underground or on the surface at a distance from the original plant:

> The world has become chaos, but the book remains the image of the world: radicle-chaosmos rather than root-cosmos. . . . A system of this kind could be called a rhizome. A rhizome as subterranean stem is absolutely different from roots and radicles. Bulbs and tubers are rhizomes. Plants with roots or radicles may be rhizomorphic in other respects altogether: the question is whether plant life in its specificity is not entirely

rhizomatic. Even some animals are, in their pack form. Rats are rhizomes. Burrows are too, in all of their functions of shelter, supply, movement, evasion, and breakout. The rhizome itself assumes very diverse forms, from ramified surface extension in all directions to concretion into bulbs and tubers. When rats swarm over each other. The rhizome includes the best and the worst: potato and couchgrass, or the weed. Animal and plant, couchgrass is crabgrass. (TP, 6-7)

All this botanical detail sets up the paradigm Deleuze and Guattari want to use as a means of mapping social structures, including especially always multiple languages as essential features of those structures:

A rhizome ceaselessly establishes connections between semiotic chains, organizations of power, and circumstances relative to the arts, sciences, and social struggles. A semiotic chain is like a tuber agglomerating very diverse acts, not only linguistic, but also perceptive, mimetic, gestural and cognitive: there is no language in itself, nor are there any linguistic universals, only a throng of dialects, patois, slangs, and specialized languages. There is no ideal speaker-listener, any more than there is a homogeneous linguistic community. Language is, in Weinreich's words, "an essentially heterogeneous reality."[32] There is no mother tongue, only a power takeover by a dominant language within a political multiplicity. Language stabilizes around a parish, a bishopric, a capital. It forms a bulb. It evolves by subterranean stems and flows, along river valleys or train tracks: it spreads like a patch of oil. (TP, 7)

Deleuze and Guattari attempt to sidestep the organic implications of the rhizome as model by speaking of heterogeneity and of the machinal proliferation of rhizomatic structures. They speak of "the *abstract machine* that connects a language to the semantic and pragmatic contents of statements, to collective assemblages of enunciation, to a whole micropolitics of the social field" (TP, 7). I think it is difficult, however, to get away completely, if one uses the word "rhizome" at all, even in a somewhat twisted or "anasemic" way, from the fact that a rhizome is an organic copy of its parent plant. Nevertheless, Deleuze and Guattari use the rhizome model brilliantly in many provocative ways. Among them is the way the rhizome presides from the first page on over their way of reading Kafka in *Kafka: Toward a Minor Literature*.³³ Kafka's work, they say in the first sentence of this book, is "a rhizome, a burrow" (3). They go on immediately to exemplify this claim with three examples, the castle in *The Castle*, the hotel in *Amerika*, and the burrow in "The Burrow":

> How can we enter into Kafka's work? This work is a rhizome, a burrow. The castle has multiple entrances whose rules of usage and whose locations aren't very well known. The hotel in *Amerika* has innumerable main doors and side doors that innumerable guards watch over; it even has entrances and exits without doors. Yet it might seem that the burrow in the story of that name has only one entrance; the most the animal can do is dream of a second entrance that would serve only for surveillance. But this is a trap arranged by the animal and by Kafka himself; the whole description of the burrow functions to trick the enemy. . . . Only the principle of multiple entrances prevents the introduction of the enemy, the Signifier and those attempts to interpret a work that is actually only open to experimentation. (K, 3)

I conclude this chapter by noting that Deleuze and Guattari's model is spatial. It thinks of Kafka's works as each generating in the reader the vision of an imaginary and extremely peculiar space, like that of the burrow in *"Der Bau"* ("The Burrow"), so elaborately described by the animal that has made it and that lives in it. I shall keep this rhizomatic spatial model in mind, along with the other models of community explored in this chapter, in my readings of Kafka's three novels and in subsequent chapters too. The spatial paradigms I derive from my novels, however, are somewhat different, as you will see.

Notes

1. Jean-Luc Nancy, *La communauté désoeuvré* (Paris: Christian Bourgois, 2004), 11, henceforth CD, followed by the page number.

2. Jean-Luc Nancy, *The Inoperative Community,* ed. Peter Connor, trans. Peter Connor, Lisa Garbus, Michael Holland, and Simona Sawney (Minneapolis: University of Minnesota Press, 1991), 1, trans. modified, henceforth IC, followed by the page number.

3. Wallace Stevens, *The Collected Poems* (New York: Vintage, 1990), 418-19, henceforth CP, followed by the page number.

4. Translator's note in Jean-Luc Nancy, *Being Singular Plural,* trans. Robert D. Richardson and Anne E. O'Byrne (Stanford: Stanford University Press, 2000), 201, henceforth BSP. The OED defines the word as 1) "to appear, make one's appearance, show one's face, esp. at a formal assembly," and as 2) "to appear in a court, as a party to a cause, either in person or by counsel."

5. Here are references to some of these: Benedict Anderson, *Imagined Communities: Reflections on the Origin and Spread of Nationalism* (New York: Random House, 1983); Jean-Luc Nancy, *Être singulier pluriel* (Paris: Galilée, 1996), henceforth ESP; Jean-Luc Nancy, *Being Singular Plural,* see footnote 4; Georges Bataille, *L'Apprenti Sorcier du cercle communiste démocratique à Acéphale : textes, lettres et documents* (1932-1939), ed. Marina Galletti; notes trans. from Italian by Natália Vital (Paris: Éditions de la Différence, 1999); Maurice Blanchot, *La communauté inavouable* (Paris: Minuit, 1983); Maurice Blanchot, *The Inavowable Community,* trans. Pierre Joris (Barrytown, N. Y.: Station Hill Press, 1988); Giorgio Agamben, *La comunità che viene* (Turin: Einaudi, 1990); Giorgio Agamben, *The Coming Community,* trans. Michael Hardt (Minneapolis: University of Minnesota Press, 1993); Alphonso Lingis, *The Community of Those Who Have Nothing in Common* (Bloomington: Indiana University Press, 1994).

6. For English translations of these essays see Martin Heidegger, "Building Dwelling Thinking," *Poetry, Language, Thought,* trans. Albert Hofstadter (New York: Harper & Row, 1971), 143-61; ibid., *Elucidations of Hölderlin's Poetry,* trans. Keith Hoeller (New York: Humanity Books, 2000. For the German originals see Martin Heidegger, *"Bauen Wohenen Denken," Vorträge und Aufsätze,* 2 (Pfullingen: Neske, 1967), 19-36; ibid. *Erläuterungen zu Hölderlins Dichtung,* 2nd ed., (Frankfurt am Main: Vittorio Klostermann, 1951).

7. Jennifer Bajorek, "The Offices of Homeland Security, or, Hölderlin's Terrorism," *Critical Inquiry,* 31, 4 (2005), 874-902.

8. See W. B. Yeats, "A Prayer for My Daughter," *The Variorum Edition of the Poems,* 7th printing, ed. Peter Allt and Russell K. Alspach (New York: Macmillan, 1977), 405.

9. Cited from online PDF of *Critical Inquiry* essay, no pagination.

10. I have discussed Nancy's concept of community briefly from the perspective of its contrast with Derrida's idea of (non)community in "Derrida Enisled,"

chapter six of my *For Derrida* (New York: Fordham University Press, 2009), 119-20.

11. Jacques Derrida, *A Taste for the Secret*, with Maurizio Ferraris, trans. Giacomo Donis, ed. Giacomo Donis and David Webb (Cambridge: Polity, 2001), 25.

12. Jean-Luc Nancy, *Le partage des voix* (Paris: Galilée, 1982).

13. Yet a third book on community by Nancy, *La communauté affrontée* (Paris: Galilée, 2001), extends but does not contradict what he says in the two much longer books.

14. Matthew Arnold, *The Poems*, ed. Kenneth Allott (London: Longmans, 1965), 242.

15. Charles Baudelaire, "*Au lecteur*," *Fleurs du mal*, *Oeuvres completes*, Pléiade ed., ed. Y.-G. le Dantec (Paris: Gallimard, 1954), 82.

16. Marurice Blanchot, *The Unavowable Community*, ed. cit., 42-3. A longer passage on the previous page can serve as a gloss or preparation for the paragraph about Tristan and Isolde. Blanchot is speaking about the relation between the two lovers in Marguerite Duras's *La maladie de la mort* (*The Malady of Death*):

    . . . in the homogeneity—the affirmation of the Same—understanding demands that the heterogeneous appear suddenly, i.e., the absolute Other in terms of which any relationship signifies: no relationship, the impossibility that willing and perhaps even desire ever cross the uncrossable, in the sudden and clandestine meeting (outside of time) that annuls itself with the devastating feeling that is never certain to be experienced by the one whom this movement consigns to the other perhaps by depriving him of his "self." A devastating feeling that is, in truth, beyond all feeling, ignoring pathos, overflowing consciousness, breaking with self-involvement and demanding—without rights—that which removes itself from all demands, because in my request there is not only the beyond of what could satisfy it, but the beyond of what is requested. An overbidding, an outrage of life that cannot be contained within life and which thus, interrupting the pretension of always persevering in being, opens to the strangeness of an interminable dying or of an endless "error." (41)

17. Jacques Derrida, *Rogues: Two Essays on Reason*, trans. Pascale-Anne Barault and Michael Nass (Stanford, Calif.: Stanford University Press, 2005), 60; ibid., *Voyous: Deux essays sur la raison* (Paris: Galilée, 2003), 90.

18. *La bête et le souverain (deuxième année)*, 1st seminar, my trans. from computer files in my possession.

19. See Wang Fengzhen and Shaobo Xie, "Introductory Notes: Dialogues on Globalization and Indigenous Cultures," in a special issue of *Ariel*, "Globalization and indigenous Cultures," 34: 1 (January 1903), 1-13. See also

my essay in that issue, "The Indigene and the Cybersurfer," 31-52. This present chapter adapts a good bit of material from that essay.

20. Wang Fengzhen and Shaobo Zie, "*Globalization and Indigenous Cultures.* Proposal for *Ariel* Special Issue 2003," 1.

21. *The Medium is the Maker: Browning, Freud, Derrida and the New Telepathic Technologies* (Brighton; Portland: Sussex Academic Press, 2009).

22. Mark Warschauer, "Demystifying the Digital Divide," *Scientific American* (August, 2003). 42-7. (Last accessed online November 2009)

23. Hayles's abundant and widely influential work goes from *How We Became Posthuman: Virtual Bodies in Cybernetics, Literature, and Informatics* (Chicago: University of Chicago Press, 1999) to *My Mother Was a Computer* (Chicago: University of Chicago Press, 2005), and *Electronic Literature: New Horizons for the Literary* (Notre Dame: University of Notre Dame Press, 2008). For Donna Haraway, see *Simians, Cyborgs, and Women: The Reinvention of Nature* (New York: Routledge, 1991). For Derrida, see *Papier Machine* (Paris: Galilée, 2001); *ibid.*, *Paper Machine*, trans. Rachel Bowlby (Stanford, Calif.: Stanford University Press, 2005). For a collection of essays about the intermediations of print technologies, film technologies, and digital technologies, see *Animated Writing: Literature, Film, Digitality*, ed. Kiene Brillenburg Wurth, forthcoming from Fordham University Press. This book contains abundant references to the immense literature that already exists on these topics. One somewhat disquieting sign of globalization is that the essays in this book are all in English, though many of the authors appear to have English as a second language.

24. Cited by from Foucault's *Power/Knowledge* by Giorgio Agamben in an essay on Foucault, "What Is an Apparatus," *What Is an Apparatus? And Other Essays*, trans David Kishik and Stefan Pedatella (Stanford, California: Stanford University Press, 2009), 2. This paragraph and the next appropriate, modify, and extend sentences from an as yet unpublished essay of mine, "Anachronistic Reading."

25. Franz Kafka, *The Office Writings*, ed. Stanley Corngold, Jack Greenberg, and Benno Wagner, trans. Eric Patton with Ruth Hein (Princeton, N. J.: Princeton University Press, 2009). Both Wallace Stevens and Franz Kafka, by a strange happenstance, were high level lawyers in accident insurance companies. Stevens worked as a Vice President for the Hartford Accident and Indemnity Company. On the one hand, Kafka's office writings are fascinating, as are the commentaries and factual data the editors provide. Here are documents the great creative writer Franz Kafka wrote as a busy lawyer in a huge governmental bureaucracy. The editors are right to seek and to find parallels with Kafka's fictional writings, diaries, and letters. On the other hand, these writings with their endless nitpicking legal detail are bewildering and, it must be said, boring, like most bureaucratic documents, just as are, in their own

way, the lengthy statements to Joseph K. made by the lawyer, Huld, and by the artist, Titorelli, in *The Trial*, though Joseph K.'s life depends on listening carefully, and to K. by Bürgel in *The Castle*. Bürgel's virtually endless and overscrupulous account of the responsibilities and evasions of responsibility of castle officials puts K. to sleep, though if he had listened, he might have found a way to the castle after all. All these scenes have their grimly comic side.

26. Louis Althusser, "Ideology and Ideological State Apparatuses (Notes Towards an Investigation)," in *Lenin and Philosophy and Other Essays*, trans. Ben Brewster (New York: Monthly Review Press, 1972).

27. Stanley Fish, *Is There a Text in This Class? The Authority of Interpretive Communities* (Cambridge, Mass.: Harvard University Press, 1980).

28. Jacques Derrida, *L'université sans condition* (Paris: Galilée, 2001); ibid, "The University without Condition," trans. Peggy Kamuf, in *Without Alibi*, ed. and trans. Peggy Kamuf (Stanford, Calif.: Stanford University Press, 2002), 202-37.

29. Derrida, *The University without Condition*, see especially pp. 130-1.

30. Derrida, *A Taste for the Secret*, 27. "Gregge" is of course related to the English word "gregarious." Derrida here claims he is not gregarious.

31. Gilles Deleuze and Félix Guattari, *A Thousand Plateaus: Capitalism and Schizophrenia*, trans. Brian Massumi (Minneapolis: University of Minnesota Press, 1987). Henceforth TP, followed by the page number.

32. U. Weinreich, W. Labov, and M. Herzog, "Empirical Foundations for a Theory of Language," in W. Lehmann and Y. Malkeiel, eds., *Directions for Historical Linguistics* (Austin: University of Texas Press, 1968), 125.

33. Gilles Deleuze and Félix Guattari, *Kafka: Toward a Minor Literature*, trans. Dana Polan (Minneapolis: University of Minnesota Press, 1986). Henceforth K, followed by the page number.

VI

Globalization and World Literature

And fast by hanging in a golden Chain
This pendant world, in bigness as a Starr
Of smallest magnitude close by the Moon.
Thither full fraught with mischievous revenge,
Accurst, and in a cursed hour he hies.
...
... [Satan] toward the coast of Earth beneath,
Down from th'Ecliptic, sped with hop'd success,
Throws his steep flight in many an Aerie wheele,
Nor staid, till on *Niphates* top he lights.

John Milton, *Paradise Lost*, II: 1051-1055;
III: 739-742 [Milton, 1674]

World literature in its recently resurrected form is indubitably a concomitant of economic and financial globalization, as well as of new world-wide telecommunications. Marx and Engels long ago, in a famous passage in the *Communist Manifesto* (1948), prophetically said just that: "And as in material, so also in intellectual production. The intellectual creations of individual nations become common property. National one-sidedness and narrow-mindedness become more and more impossible, and from the numerous national and local literatures there arises a world literature." ("Und wie in der materiellen, so auch in der geistigen Produktion. Die geistigen Erzeugnisse der einzelnen Nationen werden Gemeingut. Die nationale Einseitigkeit und Beschränktheit wird mehr und mehr unmöglich, und aus den vielen nationalen und lokalen Literaturen bildet sich eine Weltliteratur.") (Marx and Engels, 1848). We are on all sides asked by the media to think globally and given information about globalization in its current form. We have also been granted for the first time in human history an ability to look at the earth from outer space, that is, from outside what is happening here. Millions of people all over the world have seen one or another of the unsettling space-ship or satellite photographs. They provide a distant and detached perspective on the earth with a vengeance. To be, or to pretend to be, wholly detached and objective is, nevertheless, perhaps diabolical. John Milton imagined Satan as one of the first space-travellers in literature, as in the passages from early in *Paradise Lost* I have begun by citing.[1] Satan was not exactly detached, since his goal was to bring about the fall of man, but he certainly could see the whole earth from a distance, hanging in space, as all the sons and daughters of Eve can do nowadays. We are not exactly detached and indifferent either.

World Literature's time has come (again). The new World Literature is a concomitant of current globalization. I strongly support the project of World Literature.[2] The present context for developing a rigorous discipline of world literature is, however, quite different from, for example, the context in which Goethe two centuries ago proposed the reading of *Weltliteratur*. Our present context includes the many facets of globalization today: worldwide economic and cultural interaction; unprecedented travel and migration; a world-wide financial crisis made possible by the global interconnection of banks and other financial institutions; humanly-caused climate change that is altering life both human and nonhuman worldwide and that may even lead to the extinction of the species *homo sapiens*; the development of new teletechnologies like the computer, cellphones, email, the Internet, Facebook, and Twitter. These communication devices connect people all over the world in unprecedented ways.

The recent impressive development of a new discipline called "World Literature" seems pretty far from climate change, the World Wide Web, and the financial meltdown, but I think it can be shown to be a somewhat different version of a pattern of inadvertent reversal evident in those forms of globalization. The renewed emphasis on the teaching and study of world literature has without doubt been a response to manifold forms of technological and economic globalization. Another quite different response is the widespread takeover of literature departments by those kinds of social studies called "cultural studies," "postcolonial studies," "ethnic studies," "women's studies," "film studies," and so on. These developments also seem to me a good thing. It is harder and harder to justify the separate study of a supposedly homogeneous national literature, or to justify the isolated study of literature separately from other cultural forms. Widespread migration from all over the world to all over the world has meant that more and more people worldwide live in ethnically diverse communities where many languages are spoken, if you can any longer call them communities. In one section of Montreal in Canada, I am told, an astonishing 56 different languages are spoken. It seems natural and inevitable these days to look at literature globally.

Doing that, however, differs radically from the shift to cultural studies and their ilk. The latter tend to take for granted that print literature is playing a smaller and smaller role in most people's lives, as new media like film, television, Face Book, and computer games replace printed novels, plays, and poems.

The ethos of fewer and fewer people worldwide is determined to any large extent by reading "literature" in the traditional Western sense of printed novels, poems, and plays. This transformation is no doubt occurring unevenly around the globe, but it is happening to some degree everywhere. I wish this were not so, but the evidence shows that it is the case. Statistical evidence shows the astounding number of hours a day many people spend surfing the Web or using a cell-phone. People these days use the Net, talk or text on their iPhones, send emails, play computer games, listen to MP3 music, go to the movies, or watch television, all worthy activities. They do everything, however, but read Shakespeare or Jane Austen. Literature in the old-fashioned sense, such of it as is left, is migrating to e-readers like Amazon's Kindle or Apple's iPad. Amazon now sells more e-books than hardcover printed books.

Literature in the traditional sense tends to be marginalized in cultural studies, as it is in the lives of the mostly younger scholar-teachers who "do cultural studies." The new discipline of World Literature, on the contrary, might be seen as a last ditch effort to rescue the study of literature. It does this by implicitly claiming that studying literature from around the world is a way to understand globalization. This understanding allows one to become a citizen of the world, a cosmopolitan, not just a citizen of this or that local monolingual community. In the course of developing the new World Literature, however—through the planning of courses, the publication of textbooks, and the training of competent teachers—some problems arise. Here are three important challenges to the new world literature:

One: The challenge of translation. No single student, teacher, or ordinary reader can master all the hundreds of languages in which world literature is written. Any literary work can be translated into any language, but difficulties of translation always exist. Will world literature have a single master language, such as Chinese or English, into which a given textbook will translate all the selections? That would appear to be a form of cultural imperialism. How can world literature avoid being dominated by some single national academic culture?

Two: The challenge of representation. A scholar can spend his or her whole life studying a single national literature and still not master it. World literature will of necessity, for example in textbooks or courses, work by way of relatively brief selections from the literature of many countries or regions. Such selections will always be to some degree biased or controversial. How can this bias be avoided as much as possible? Who will have the authority to decide which works in a given language or in a given national literature belong to world literature? What will be the criteria for the decisions to include or exclude? Does Franz Kafka, for example, belong to world literature? The book on Kafka by Gilles Deleuze and Félix Guattari is subtitled *Toward a Minor Literature* (Deleuze and Guattari, 1986). Is that a true description? Does being "minor" mean Kafka's works do not belong to "world literature"? How would you know for sure one way or the other?

David Damrosch, in the brilliant introductory essay to his *What Is World Literature?* (Damrosch, 2003, 1-36), touches with wisdom and impressive learning on all the issues I am raising. He sidesteps the problem of setting a canon of world literature by saying that "world literature is not an infinite, ungraspable canon of works but rather a mode of circulation and of reading" (Damrosch, 2003, 5). Teachers of World Literature and editors of textbooks on World Literature still need to decide, however, which works to help circulate and get read. Such experts also need to decide what to tell students about a work from a culture that is different from their own. Damrosch identifies succinctly the challenges to doing this. "A specialist in classical Chinese poetry," he says, "can gradually, over years of labor, develop a close familiarity with the vast substratum beneath each brief T'ang Dynasty poem, but most of this context is lost to foreign readers when the poem travels abroad. Lacking specialized knowledge, the foreign reader is likely to impose domestic literary values on the foreign work, and even careful scholarly attempts to read a foreign work in light of a Western critical theory are deeply problematic" (Damrosch, 2003, 4-5).

Three: The challenge of defining what is meant by "literature." Goethe, in one of those famous conversations with Eckermann about world literature, serenely affirms his belief that "literature" is a universal, something possessed by every human culture everywhere at all times. When Eckermann, Goethe's fall guy or straight man, resisted reading Chinese novels by asking whether the one they have been discussing is "perhaps one of their most superior ones," Goethe responded firmly:

> "By no means," said Goethe; "the Chinese have thousands of them, and had when our forefathers were still living in the woods.
>
> "I am more and more convinced," he continued, "that poetry is the universal possession of mankind. . . . the epoch of world literature is at hand, and everyone must strive to hasten its approach." (Goethe, 1930, 132)

Even within a relatively homogeneous, though multilingual, culture, such as that of Western Europe and America, "literature" is not quite so easy to define or to take for granted as Goethe makes it sound. Nonetheless, one might say of literature what a United States Supreme Court Justice famously said about pornography: "I can't define it, but I know it when I see it." Literature in its modern Western form is not even three centuries old. Is it legitimate to globalize that parochial notion of what is meant by "literature"? The modern Western idea of literature is parochial in the sense of being limited to Western culture during one historical time—the time of the rise of the middle class, of increasing literacy, and of the printed book. It seems unlikely that what we Westerners have meant by "literature" for the last couple of centuries would hold true worldwide. How can a discipline of World Literature respect the many different conceptions of "literature" in different times and places throughout the world? Damrosch recognizes that "literature" means something different in each culture, but he says we can define literature as whatever people in diverse times and places take as literature. All of us, in all our diversity of cultures and conceptions of literature, know a piece of literature when we see one.

The effort to globalize literary study, admirable as it is, encounters through its deployment intrinsic features in so-called literature that unglobalize the project. These features of diversity tend, or ought to tend, to return literary study not so much to the dispersed and self-enclosed investigations of national literatures in a given language in a given time and place as to the one by one reading of individual works that we have decided are examples of literature. The narrowness and parochialism of segregated national literature study is just what the redevelopment of World Literature was trying to escape. Comprehensive study of even a single national literature, however, is a Herculean, perhaps impossible, task. In the end no literary work, it may be, fits the periodizing or generic generalizations that can be made about it. To speak of "the Victorian novel" is a mystified projection of unity where immense variation actually exists.

The new discipline of World Literature, I conclude, problematizes itself, or ought to problematize itself, through rigorous investigation of the presuppositions that made the development of World Literature as an academic discipline possible and desirable in the first place. Does that mean it is not worthwhile to read a few pages of Chinese, Kenyan, or Czech literature in English translation, with succinct expert commentary? Would it be better not to read bits of those literatures at all? By no means. The challenges to world literature I have identified do mean, however, that one should not exaggerate the degree to which courses in World Literature are any more than a valuable first step toward giving students global knowledge of literatures and cultures from all corners of the earth.

I turn now to a thought experiment. Suppose I were a Chinese scholar preparing a textbook in Chinese of world literature. Suppose, furthermore, that I had decided, for whatever reason, to include a translation into Chinese of W. B. Yeats's "The Cold Heaven" in my textbook. This short lyric is from Yeats's volume of 1916, *Responsibilities*. Just what would I need to tell Chinese readers to make them the best possible readers of this poem? Here is the poem. I choose it because I greatly admire it and find it immensely moving. It is available in a number of sites online.

The Cold Heaven

Suddenly I saw the cold and rook-delighting heaven
That seemed as though ice burned and was but the more ice,
And thereupon imagination and heart were driven
So wild that every casual thought of that and this
Vanished, and left but memories, that should be out of season
With the hot blood of youth, of love crossed long ago;
And I took all the blame out of all sense and reason,
Until I cried and trembled and rocked to and fro,
Riddled with light. Ah! when the ghost begins to quicken,
Confusion of the death-bed over, is it sent
Out naked on the roads, as the books say, and stricken
By the injustice of the skies for punishment? (Yeats, 1977, 316.)[3]

I list, in an order following that of the poem, some of the things that might need to be explained not only to a Chinese reader, but also, no doubt, to a computer-games-playing Western young person ignorant of European poetry. David Damrosch recognizes with equanimity, as do I, that when a given piece of literature circulates into a different culture from that of its origin, it will be read differently. I am not talking here, however, about a high-level culturally embedded reading, but just about making sense of Yeats's poem. This need to make sense might arise, for example, in trying to decide how to translate this or that phrase into Chinese. Here are some things it might be good to know when trying to understand "The Cold Heaven": 1) Something about Yeats's life and works; 2) An explanation of the verse form used: three iambic hexameter quatrains rhyming abab. Is it an odd sort of sonnet in hexameters rather than in pentameters, and missing the last couplet? ; 3) Knowledge of the recurrent use of "sudden" or "suddenly" in Yeats's lyrics; 4) What sort of bird a rook is and why they are delighted by cold weather; 5) The double meaning of "heaven," as "skies" and as the supernatural realm beyond the skies, as in the opening of the Lord's Prayer, said daily by millions of Christians: "Our Father who art in heaven"; compare "skies" at the end: "the injustice of the skies for punishment"; 6) An explanation of oxymorons (e.g. burning ice) and of the history in Western poetry of this particular one; 7) Attempt to explain the semantic difference between "imagination" and "heart," as well as the nuances of each word ; 8) Explanation of "crossed" in "memories . . . of love crossed long ago," both the allusion to Shakespeare's Romeo and Juliet as "star-cross'd lovers" (Shakespeare, 1597, Prologue, 6), that is, as fated by the stars to disaster in love, and the reference to the biographical fact of Yeats's disastrous love for Maud Gonne: she turned him down repeatedly, so it is to some degree absurd for him to take responsibility for the failure of their love; he did his best to woo her; 9) Account of the difference between "sense" and "reason" in "I took the blame out of all sense and reason," or is this just tautological? A. Norman Jeffares cites T. R. Henn's explanation that "'out of all sense' is an Irish (and ambiguous) expression meaning both 'to an extent far beyond what common sense could justify' and 'beyond the reach of sensation'" (Jeffares. 1968, 146); 10) Explanation of the double meaning of the verb "riddle" in the marvelous phrase, "riddled with light": "riddle" as an adjective meaning puncture with holes and "riddle" (A "riddle" is a kind of sieve.), and as a verb meaning having a perhaps unanswered riddle or conundrum posed to one; being riddled with light is paradoxical because light is supposed to be illuminating, not obscuring; 11) Unsnarling of the lines centering on "quicken" in "when the ghost [meaning disembodied soul] begins to quicken,/Confusion of the death bed over"; "quicken" usually refers to the coming to life of the fertilized egg in the womb, so an erotic love-bed scene is superimposed on the death-bed one; 12) "as the books say": which books? The esoteric and Irish folklore ones Yeats delighted in; 13) Relate "injustice of the skies for punishment" to the usual assumption that heaven only punishes justly, gives us our just deserts after death; why and how can the skies be unjust? By blaming him for something that was not his fault? Relate this to Greek and later tragedy. It is not Oedipus's fault that he has killed his father and fathered children on his mother, or is it? Are we all guilty? 14) Why is the last sentence a question? Is it a real question or a merely rhetorical one? Would the answer find its place if the blank that follows the twelve lines of this defective sonnet were filled? The poem seems both too much in line lengths and too little in number of lines. 15) Finally, Chinese readers might like to know, or might even observe on their own, that Yeats, like other European poets of his generation, was influenced in this poem and elsewhere by what he knew, through translations, of Chinese poetry and Chinese ways of thinking. The volume *Responsibilities*, which contains "The Cold Heaven," has an epigraph from someone Yeats calls, somewhat pretentiously, "Khoung-Fou-Tseu," presumably Confucius: "How am I fallen from myself, for a long time now/I have not seen the Prince of Chang in my dreams" (Yeats, 1977, 269). Chinese readers might have a lot to say about this Chinese connection and about how it makes "The Cold Heaven" a work of world literature.

I have stressed the challenges and difficulties faced by world literature as a discipline concomitant with the new forms of globalization. That does not mean world literature should not flourish. Shakespeare, in the various plots of *As You Like It* (Shakespeare, 1600), shows pretty conclusively that love in the sense of sexual desire and love in the sense of spiritual affection may not by any means be reconciled. They form an aporia, an impasse. No bringing together of lust and love. The play ends triumphantly, however, with four marriages. These break through the impasse. Let world literature thrive, say I, just as Shakespeare's mad King Lear says, "Let copulation thrive" (*Shakespeare*, 1606, IV, 6, 116).

ૐ

As I expected, I learned much from all the papers at the Shanghai conference on "Comparative Literature in the Phase of World Literature: The Fifth Sino-American Symposium on Comparative Literature" (August 11-15, 2010). By meeting and hearing so many of the leaders worldwide in the revived discipline of World Literature, I learned that World Literature is thriving globally and that a consensus is beginning to emerge about what World Literature is and what it does, what its conventions and protocols are.

I found especially relevant to my own reflections about World Literature Thomas Beebee's paper asking "What in the World does Friedrich Nietzsche have against *Weltliteratur?*" I found Professor Beebee's paper extremely provocative, not least by way of the citations from Nietzsche's *The Birth of Tragedy* and *Beyond Good and Evil* the exegesis of which generated his essay. I had so much to say about both Beebee's paper and the citations on his handout that I refrained from commenting at the time he presented his paper from fear of impolitely taking up too much time in the discussion. The following remarks are no more than an extended footnote to Thomas Beebee's admirable paper.

Just what does Nietzsche have against *Weltliteratur*? In order to be brief and to avoid an interminable exegesis, I limit myself almost completely to the citations in Beebee's handout. Readers of the major essays on *The Birth of Tragedy* by Paul de Man (de Man, 1979, 79-101), Andrzej Warminski (Warminski, 1987; Warminski, 1989), Carol Jacobs (Jacobs, 1978), and Thomas Albrecht (Albrecht, 2009), will know how complex, contradictory, and controversial *The Birth of Tragedy* is. Warminski, in "Reading for Example," for example, gives an example of the problems of translation I have mentioned. He shows that Walter Kaufmann, in the standard translation of *The Birth of Tragedy*, misleadingly translates the German word *Gleichnis* as "symbol," thereby importing the whole Romantic ideology of symbol into Nietzsche's text, whereas *Gleichnis* actually means "parable," or "figure," or "image" (Warminski, 1987, xliv-xlv).

What Nietzsche says in the striking passage from *The Birth of Tragedy* Beebee began by citing adds one more challenge to the enterprise of World Literature to the three I identify and discuss above. Readers of Nietzsche's "*Vom Nutzen und Nachtheil der Historie für das Leben*" (Nietzsche, 1988b) ("On the Advantage and Disadvantage of History for Life" [Nietzsche, 1995]; the translation I cite uses a different title) will remember that Nietzsche argues, paradoxically and even scandalously, that it is healthy to forget history so we can get on with living productively in the present, starting afresh without the great weight of history on our shoulders. The title has been translated in many different ways, in exemplification of what I say above about translation and World Literature, but my German dictionary gives "advantage" and "disadvantage" as the primary meanings of *Nutz* and *Nachtheil*. This essay is Nietzsche's version of James Joyce's definition of history as "the nightmare from which I am trying to awake." Nietzsche's and Joyce's view of history seems paradoxical and scandalous, I mean, to us humanities professors who have given our lives to studying the history of literature, including for many now World Literature. Nietzsche himself was charged with an obligation study literary history as an Ordinarius Professor of Classical Philology at the University of Basle. Appointed at twenty-four, he was one of the youngest ever called to such a post. The Nietzschean view is the opposite of the by no means implausible counter-assertion that those who forget history are condemned to repeat it.

Nietzsche's basic assumption, in the extracts from *The Birth of Tragedy* and *Beyond Good and Evil* Beebee discusses, is that we now live trapped in the meshes of an Alexandrian culture: "Our whole modern world is entangled in the net of Alexandrian culture (*in dem Netz der alexandrinischen Cultur befangen*). It proposes as its ideal the theoretical man equipped with the greatest forces of knowledge (*Erkenntnisskräften*), and laboring in the service of science (*Wissenschaft*), whose archetype and progenitor is Socrates" (Nietzsche, 1967, 110; Nietzsche, 1988a, 116). Just what do these two sentences mean? They mean that, like the citizens of Alexandria in the twilight of the ancient Greek world, we in the modern world know everything and have accumulated all knowledge, such as was gathered in the famous Library of Alexandria, or as was collected the great European university libraries of Nietzsche's time, or as does the Internet encompass today. In these days of global telecommunications, you can get information about almost anything by Googling it from almost anywhere in the world. Moreover, even our art, as Nietzsche repeatedly emphasizes, has been enfeebled by becoming imitative, by being cut off from fresh sources of inspiration. Our poets and artists know too much about the histories of poetry and art. This is Nietzsche's version of what Harold Bloom, in the late twentieth century, was to call "the anxiety of influence" (Bloom, 1973).

Nietzsche takes a dim view of this. Why? Why does Nietzsche define the power of knowing everything as like being entangled in a net? It might seem a wonderful asset to have knowledge of everything under the sun at one's fingertips. On the contrary, Nietzsche holds that just as a wild animal, a fish, or a bird caught in a net is deprived of the ability to live its life freely, so Alexandrian people are paralyzed, prevented from living a normal human life, by knowing too much. Nietzsche concept of a proper human life is to live and act in the present, in a particular situation and oriented toward the future, forgetting the past. One of Beebee's citations quotes Nietzsche praising Napoleon to Eckermann as the type of the non-theoretical man who embodies "a productiveness of deeds" ("*eine Productivität der Thaten*") (Nietzsche, 1967, 111; Nietzsche, 1988a, 116). Normal human beings dwell within a local culture. This culture includes indigenous literature and other art forms. Such a culture is sequestered from other cultures and takes its assumptions, as well as its native language, as universals. The Greeks saw everyone who did not speak Greek as "barbarians." It sounded as if they were stammering "bar...bar...bar," not speaking anything intelligible. Learning another language seemed pointless or dangerous to the Greeks. It would lead to dissonance, to the multiplication and dissolution of the self.

The word "dissonance" appears in the second of Beebee's citations. It is taken from the last section of *The Birth of Tragedy*, section twenty-five. The word "dissonance" appears with increasing frequency toward the end of *The Birth of Tragedy*. "If we could imagine dissonance become man (*eine Menschwerdung der Dissonanz*)—and what else is man?—this dissonance, to be able to live, would need a splendid illusion (*eine herrliche Illusion*) that would cover dissonance with a veil of beauty (*einen Schönheitsschleier über ihr eignes Wesen*)" (Nietzsche, 1967, 143; Nietzsche, 1988a, 155), A more literal translation would say "spread a veil of beauty over its own being." "*Ihr* (its)" could refer either to dissonance or to man, but Nietzsche's argument, after all, is that man is essentially dissonance. They are the same. Man is dissonance in living human form. (Present-day readers are likely to note, by the way, the imperturbable sexism of Nietzsche's formulations. He speaks of dissonance become man, not man and woman. *Mensch* apparently includes everyone, both men and women. Sexual difference does not matter to Nietzsche, at least not in these citations. "Birth [*Geburt*]" is used in the title without apparent reference to the fact that only women can give birth.)

Just what is Nietzsche's "dissonance"? Thomas Beebee was perhaps too reticent or too intellectually chaste to say anything, so far as I can remember his oral presentation, about that dissonant can of worms, the vexed opposition between the Dionysian and the Apollinian that ambiguously organizes the whole of *The Birth of Tragedy*. That opposition is especially salient as the leitmotif of section twenty-five. In incautiously opening that can of worms, I say the opposition "ambiguously" organizes *The Birth of Tragedy* because though at first it seems that the Dionysian and the Apollonian are in clear opposition, it turns out that matters are not quite so simple. The Dionysian, it appears, refers to the underlying cacophony of the universal Will, "the Dionysian basic ground of the world (*dionysischen Untergrund der Welt*)" (Nietzsche, 1967, 143; Nietzsche, 1988a, 155). Music and Greek tragedy (Sophocles and Aeschylus, but not Euripides) are direct expressions of this Dionysian "basic ground of all existence (*Fundamente aller Existenz*)" (Nietzsche, 1967, 143; Nietzsche, 1988a, 155): "Music and tragic myth are equally expressions of the Dionysian capacity of a people (*der dionysischen Befähigung eines Volkes*), and they are inseparable (*untrennbar*)" (Nietzsche, 1867, 143; Nietzsche, 1988a, 154).

The full title of Nietzsche's book, after all, is "The Birth of Tragedy Out of the Spirit of Music." ("*Die Geburt der Tragödie aus dem Geiste der Musik*"). Just why Nietzsche says "spirit of music" rather than just "music" is a difficult question to answer. Apparently the spirit of music precedes actual musical compositions, such as those operas by Wagner that are Nietzsche's prime example of the modern Dionysian. The spirit of music and music, it is implied, are two different things. In any case, the Apollonian seems clearly opposed to the Dionysian. "Man" cannot face the Dionysian directly and go on living. It has to be covered over with a veil of beautiful illusion: "this dissonance [that is, dissonance become man in a *Menschwerdung*], in order to be able to live, would need a splendid illusion that would spread a veil of beauty over its own being." As T. S. Eliot puts this, "human kind/Cannot bear very much reality" (Eliot, T. S., 1952, 118).

This opposition seems clear enough. It has an Apollonian reasonable clarity. The more one reads carefully, however, everything Nietzsche wrote about the Dionysian and the Apollonian, including the abundant notes written prior to *The Birth of Tragedy*, Nietzsche's letters of the time, the recanting "Attempt at a Self-Criticism" written for the third edition of the book (1886), and the comments on *The Birth of Tragedy* in *Ecce Homo* (written 1888, published 1908), the more complicated matters become. The edition of 1886 even had a different title: *Die Geburt der Tragödie. Oder: Griechenthum und Pessimismus* (*The Birth of Tragedy. Or: Hellenism and Pessimism*). More and more the careful reader comes to recognize that the Dionysian and the Apollonian, even at the time of the first edition of *The Birth of Tragedy* (1872), are not opposites. They are, to borrow Jacobs' word, "stammering" permutations of one another as slightly different "transfigurations" or figurative displacements of an original dissonance that, *pace* Schophenhauer, can never be expressed directly, only figured by one or another catachresis. "Dissonance," after all, is not music but the absence of music in clashing sound, just as stammering is language that is not language but the product of a speech impediment that produces repetitive dissonant sounds. Even in section twenty-five the same word, "transfiguration (*Verklärung*)," is used to define what music, tragic myth, and Apollonian illusion all do in different ways: "Music and tragic myth are equally expression of the Dionysian capacity of a people, and they are inseparable. Both derive from a sphere of art that lies beyond the Apollonian; both transfigure a region in whose joyous chords dissonance as well as the terrible image of the world fade away charmingly (*beide verklären eine Region, in deren Lustaccorden die Dissonanz eben so wie das schrecklicke Weltbild reizvoll verklingt*)" (Nietzsche, 1967, 143; Nietzsche, 1988, 154). "Of this foundation of all existence—the Dionysian basic ground of the world—not one whit more may enter the consciousness of the human individual than can be overcome again by this Apollonian power of transfiguration (*apollinischen Verklärungskraft*)" (Nietzsche, 1967, 143; Nietzsche, 1988a, 155).

The reader is left in the end with an opposition not between the Dionysian and the Apollinian, but between the primordial, underlying dissonance, on the one hand, and, on the other, both the Dionysian and the Apollonian in all their various permutations as forms of the same transfiguration (in the sense of turning into figures) of what mankind cannot face directly and go on living. These apparently clear figures, however, betray their origin in their own stammering dissonance. Carol Jacobs has in her brilliant essay, ""The Stammering Text: The Fragmentary Studies Preliminary to *The Birth of Tragedy*" (Jacobs, 1978), conclusively demonstrated this in her admirable reading of the notebooks (especially notebook 9) preliminary to *The Birth of Tragedy* (Nietzsche 1988d). Her essay culminates in an exegesis of Nietzsche's use of the word "stammer (*stammeln*)" (Jacobs, 1978, 20-22) both in the notebooks and once in *The Birth of Tragedy* itself. Jacobs' difficult insight might be summarized by a slight extension of her epigraph from *The Birth of Tragedy* itself: "Thus the intricate relation of the Apollinian and the Dionysian may really be symbolized by a fraternal union of the two deities: Dionysus speaks the language of Apollo; and Apollo, finally the language of Dionysus" (*"So ware wirklich das schwierige Verhältniss des Apollinischen und des Dionysischen in der Tragödie durch einen Brunderbund beider Gottgeiten zu symbolisiren: Dionysus redet die Sprache des Apollo, Apollo aber schliesslich die Sprache des Dionysus"*) (Nietzsche, 1967, 130; Nietzsche, 1988a, 140).

In truth, Nietzsche, as Albrecht and others of the scholars listed in my footnote nine argue, saw both the Dionysian and the Apollinian as generating out of their own stammering dissonance the illusion of primordial dissonance, rather than just being figurative transfigurations of it. My word "catachresis," the tropological name for a "forced or abusive transfer," hints at this possibility.[4] I refrain from pursuing this rabbit any further down its rabbit hole. It is a good example of the way an innocent-looking word, "dissonance" in this case, like "quicken" in Yeats's "The Cold Heaven," can lead to a virtually interminable reading that ultimately includes everything the author wrote and its dissonant and therefore untotalizable intellectual, cultural, and linguistic context.

Nietzsche's harsh judgment of Goethean *Weltliteratur* is a concomitant of this larger set of contextual assumptions. Devotees of World Literature know many languages, many cultures, many literatures. They set these all next to one another in simultaneity, as exemplary of a universal or global literature that began thousands of years ago and that still flourishes everywhere in the inhabited world. The new efflorescence of world literature today is clearly a form of globalization, as I began by asserting. What Nietzsche in *Beyond Good and Evil* (1886) saw, ironically, as "civilization," "humanizing," "progress," or "the *democratic* movement in Europe" (*"Civilisation," "Vermenschlichung," "Fortschritt," "die demokratische Bewegun Europa's"*), that is, as "an immense *physiological* process . . . the slow emergence of an essentially *super-national* and nomadic species of man (*einer wesentliich übernationalen und nomadischen Art Mensch*), who possesses, physiologically speaking, a maximum of the art and power of adaptation as his typical distinction," has now in 2010 reached a hyperbolic level (I have used Beebee's unidentified translation; for the German: Nietzsche 1988c, 182). The new nomadic species of man takes many forms today, but it might be personified in the scholar who travels all over the world by jet-plane, as I do, to attend conferences and to give papers that are heard by participants who come from all over the world, the globe compacted to the size of a lecture hall.

In the light of this brief establishment of a wider context for world literature as Nietzsche saw its "disadvantage (*Nachtheil*)" for life, I now turn back to the first citation Thomas Beebee made from *The Birth of Tragedy*. The narrower context of Nietzsche's putdown of world literature is Goethe's celebration of it in that famous interchange with Eckermann about Chinese novels as a manifestation of world literature, already cited. The Chinese, Goethe told Eckermann, had novels when we Europeans were still living in the woods. "The epoch of world literature is at hand, and everyone must strive to hasten its approach," said Goethe with his usual somewhat ironic cheerfulness. It is coming anyway, so why not hasten its coming, or, rather, we *should* therefore hasten its coming. Goethe, as opposed to Nietzsche, saw no danger in world literature. In his serene and sovereign imperturbability, he welcomed its coming, perhaps because he was sure he would be part of it.

Nevertheless, the effects on Goethe's Faust of total knowledge should give the reader pause. Beebee's citations include one reference in *The Birth of Tragedy* to Goethe's Faust as the type of modern man's omniscience turning against itself in a perpetual dissatisfaction: "How unintelligible (*unverständlich*) must *Faust*, the modern cultured man, who is in himself intelligible, have appeared to a true Greek. . . . Faust, whom we have but to place bedside Socrates for the purpose of comparison, in order to see that modern man is beginning to divine the limits of this Socratic love of knowledge (*Erkenntnislust*) and yearns for a coast in the wide waste of the ocean of knowledge (*aus dem weiten wüsten Wissenmeere*)" (Nietzsche, 1967, 110-11; Nietzsche, 1988a, 116).

Well, just what does Nietzsche have against *Weltliteratur*? Here is the crucial passage Beebee cites. It must be scrutinized closely: "Our art reveals this universal distress (*diese allgemeine Noth*): in vain (*umsonst*) does one (*dass mann*) depend imitatively (*imitatorisch*) on all the great productive periods and natures; in vain does one accumulate the entire 'world-literature' around modern man for his comfort; in vain does one place oneself in the midst of the art styles and artists of all ages, so that one may give names to them as Adam did to the beasts: one still remains eternally hungry, the 'critic' without joy or energy (*ohne Lust und Kraft*), the Alexandrian man, who is at bottom a librarian and corrector of proofs, and wretchedly goes blind from the dust of books (*Bücherstaub*) and from printers' errors (*Druckfehlern*)" (Nietzsche, 1967, 113-4; Nietzsche, 1988a, 119-20). (I am myself at this moment an Alexandrian going blind from book dust and from the attempt to get all my German words spelled correctly and all the commas and numbers in my text and in my footnotes right.) Just what is the "universal distress," the unassuaged need for "comfort," the eternal hunger, which modern man suffers? The passage just cited from *The Birth of Tragedy*, as well as other passages from Nietzsche's writings, indicate that it is the distress of a successful Socratic, Faustian, or even a Kantian or Hegelian, search for total knowledge, empirically verified and epistemologically sound. This search has turned against itself through its very success. This reversal has left modern man in a state of universal distress, typified by Faust's eternal dissatisfaction. The immediate context of the passage just cited in section 18 of *The Birth of Tragedy* states this clearly, though the whole section is complex and would demand a lengthy exposition. To put what Nietzsche says in an oversimplifying nutshell, the search by "theoretical," scientific, or scholarly man for the power and equanimity granted by a comprehensive knowledge has reversed itself by reaching the irrational and illogical, from which theoretical man recoils in fear: "It is certainly a sign of the 'breach' ('*Bruches*') of which everyone speaks as the fundamental malady (*Urleiden*) of modern culture, that the theoretical man, alarmed and dissatisfied at his own consequences, no longer dares entrust himself to the terrible icy current of existence (*dem furchtbaren Eisstrome des Daseins*): he runs timidly up and down the bank.[5] So thoroughly has he been pampered by his optimistic views that he no longer wants to have anything whole (*ganz haben*), with all of nature's cruelty attaching to it. Besides, he feels that a culture based on the principles of science (*auf dem Princip der Wissenschaft*) must be destroyed when it begins to grow *illogical,* that is, to retreat (*zurück zu fliehen*) before its own consequences" (Nietzsche, 1967, 113; Nietzsche, 1988a, 119). This is the "distress (*Noth*)" of which Nietzsche speaks in the following sentence, the first in the first citation Beebee discussed: "Our art reveals this universal distress. (*Unsere Kunst offenbart diese allgemeine Noth*)."

Just how does this revelation through the art of the present moment, that is, the moment of the late nineteenth century in Europe, occur? It happens, says Nietzsche, through the Alexandrian derivative and imitative quality of today's art. Present day artists and poets know too much literary history and too much art history to produce other than feeble imitations of the great productive artists and poets of the past. Nietzsche's formulations take place through a cascade of phrases beginning with "in vain." It is as a member of this sequence that the failure of world literature to give modern man comfort in his distress is asserted: "*in vain* (*umsonst*) does one depend imitatively on all the great productive periods and natures; *in vain* does one accumulate the entire "world-literature" around modern man for his comfort (*zum Troste*); *in vain* does one place oneself in the midst of the art styles and artists of all ages, so that one may give names to them as Adam did to the beasts: one still remains eternally hungry (*der ewig Hungernde*). . . . (my italics) (Nietzsche, 1967, 113-14; Nietzsche, 1988a, 119-20)." Categorizing art styles and periods in the literature of all ages and countries (e.g. 'Baroque," "Romantic," or "Victorian"), work all we literary historians perform. is as arbitrary and ungrounded as those names Adam gave to all the beasts.

The bottom line is that for Nietzsche world literature, far from giving modern man comfort in his distress, fails completely to do that. In fact turning to world literature is one of the signal ways that distress manifests itself and is exacerbated. As far as Nietzsche is concerned, it would be better not to know, better to forget all those alien literatures that swarm around the globe. It would be better to live as Nietzsche implies Athenian Greeks did, that is, in joyful possession of a narrow local culture that ignored all other cultures and literatures and saw them as barbarous.

Nietzsche's view of Greek culture is not quite so simple, however. *The Birth of Tragedy* ends with paragraphs asserting that Athenian Apollonian beauty was a compensation for Dionysian madness: "in view of this continual influx of beauty (*diesem fortwährenden Einströmen der Schönheit*), would he [someone today imagining himself a curious stranger in ancient Athens] not have to exclaim, raising his hand to Apollo: 'Blessed people of Hellas! How great must Dionysus be among you if the god of Delos [Apollo] considers such magic necessary to heal your dithyrambic madness'" (Nietzsche, 1967, 144; Nietzsche, 1988a, 155-6). Nietzsche imagines an old Athenian responding, "But say this, too, curious stranger: how much did this people have to suffer (*leiden*) to be able to become so beautiful (*so schön*)!" (Nietzsche, 1967, 144; Nietzsche 1988a, 156).

Nietzsche's forceful rejection of world literature already manifests in hyperbolic form the reversal that was the climax of the paper I gave at the Shanghai Symposium. The new discipline of World Literature, I said, "problematizes itself, or ought to problematize itself, through rigorous investigation of the presuppositions that made the development of World Literature as an academic discipline possible and desirable in the first place." One of the bad effects of the discipline of World Literature, according to Nietzsche, is that it transforms scholars into something like what Nietzsche became or feared to become as a professor of classical philology. Nietzsche's description is memorably sardonic. It recalls George Eliot's description in *Middlemarch* of Edward Casaubon and his futile pursuit of the Key to All Mythologies. Here again is Nietzsche's description: "the 'critic' without joy or energy, the Alexandrian man, who is at bottom a librarian and corrector of proofs, and wretchedly goes blind from the dust of books and from printers' errors." It may have been in part fear of becoming like this "critic" that led Nietzsche to resign his professorship. His main overt reason was trouble with his eyesight. Here is Eliot's description of Causabon: "Poor Mr. Casaubon himself was lost among small closets and winding stairs, and in an agitated dimness about the Cabeiri [a group of Samothracian fertility gods], or in an exposure of other mythologists' ill-considered parallels, easily lost sight of any purpose which had prompted him to these labors" (Eliot, George, 1974, 229).[6] What circulates in Casaubon's veins is neither blood nor passion but marks of punctuation, just as Nietzsche's dry-as-dust scholar spends his time with misprints. As one of Casaubon's sharp-tongued neighbors, Mrs. Cadwallader, says, "Somebody put a drop [of his blood] under a magnifying-glass, and it was all semicolons and parentheses" (Eliot, George, 1974, 96). In both cases culture as enshrined in texts is reduced to the materiality of the letter or of punctuation marks, such as have preoccupied me in revising and footnoting this essay. The precociously brilliant young professor of classical philology, Friedrich Nietzsche, may have written an outrageously unorthodox first book as a way to avoid becoming just another classical philologist.

I end with one final observation. I intended to make a few brief comments about Thomas Beebee's admirable paper and about the citations from Nietzsche on which he focused. As I might have foreseen, my comments have got longer and longer and might be yet longer. They parallel the comments I made indicating what students might need to be told in order to be able to read W. B. Yeats's "The Cold Heaven." In both cases, the commentaries extend themselves indefinitely. What Thomas Beebee and then I following in his footsteps have said about Friedrich Nietzsche's theory of *Weltliteratur* indicates that theoretical statements about world literature require as much contextualizing exposition as do works of world literature themselves. Such statements must be *read*, and they must be *contextualized*.

I do not think we can ever go back to a world of isolated societies, each with its own indigenous culture. To wish we could all be like the happy ancient Athenians, as Nietzsche sometimes seems to do, is, in my view, a form of unproductive nostalgia. We must make do with what we have, which is a world-wide Alexandrian culture. The new efflorescence of World Literature as an academic discipline is a natural concomitant of this. Its great value is that even if it does not give "comfort," it does help us to understand and to live productively in the new uncomfortable world of global intercommunication and global wandering that Nietzsche calls "nomadism."

Notes

1. Claire Colebrook, in an essay entitled "A Globe of One's Own: In Praise of the Flat Earth," which I have seen in manuscript (Colebrook, 2010), sent me back to Satan's space travel in Milton. Her essay has been provocative for

me in other ways too, as have recent manuscript essays on "Critical Climate Change" by Tom Cohen.

2. I have in general capitalized "World Literature" when I mean the new discipline, not the collection of various national literatures that might be included in "world literature."

3. For a fuller discussion of the poem, see my "W. B. Yeats: 'The Cold Heaven'" in Others (Princeton, NJ: Princeton University Press, 2001), 170-182.

4. In "Reading for Example," Warminski discusses catachresis in his reading of a metaphor in *The Birth of Tragedy*. Andrzej Warminski, "Reading for Example: A Metaphor in Nietzsche's Birth of Tragedy." In *Readings in Interpretation: Hölderlin, Hegel, Heidegger* (Minneapolis: University of Minnesota Press, 1987), xxxv-lxi.

5. Here appears again the figure of the tame shore as against the dangerous ocean of universal knowledge, or, in this case, the icy current of existence. "Knowledge" and "existence" are by no means the same, however. The import of the metaphor is reversed in the second example, as happens with so much else in the language of *The Birth of Tragedy*. In the first citation, universal Socratic knowledge is seen as bad, debilitating. In the second citation, man is seen as too timid to entrust himself, as he should, to the icy waters of existence.

6. The Cabeiri were a group of Samothracian fertility gods, the notes to the Penguin *Middlemarch* tell me, with Casaubon-like learning.

Works Cited

Albrecht, Thomas. 2009. "A 'Monstrous Opposition': The Double Dionysus and the Double Apollo in Nietzsche's *Birth of* Tragedy." In The *Medusa Effect: Representation and Epistemology in Victorian Aesthetics*. Albany: State University of New York Press. 51-70.

Bloom, Harold. 1973. *The Anxiety of Influence: A Theory of Poetry*. New York: Oxford University Press.

Colebrook, Claire. 2010. "A Globe of One's Own: In Praise of the Flat Earth." Unpublished manuscript.

Damrosch, David. 2003. *What is World Literature?* Princeton: Princeton University Press.

Deleuze, Gilles, and Guattari Félix. 1986. *Kafka: Toward a Minor Literature*. Trans. Dana Polan. Minneapolis: University of Minnesota Press.

de Man Paul. 1979. "Genesis and Genealogy (*Nietzsche*)." In *Allegories of Reading: Figural Language in Rousseau. Nietzsche, Rilke, and Proust*. New Haven: Yale University Press. 79-101.

Eliot, George. 1974. *Middlemarch*. Harmondsworth, Middlesex: Penguin.

Eliot. T. S. 1952. "Burnt Norton." From *Four Quartets*. In *The Collected Poems and Plays: 1909-1950*. New York: Harcourt, Brace.

Goethe, Johann Wolfgang von. *Conversations with Eckermann*.1930. Ed. J. K. Morehead. Trans. John Oxenford. London: Everyman.

Jacobs, Carol. 1978. "The Stammering Text: The Fragmentary Studies Preliminary to *The Birth of Tragedy*." In The *Dissimulating Harmony: The Image of Interpretation in Nietzsche, Rilke, Artaud, and Benjamin*.l Baltimore: The Johns Hopkins University Press. 1-22

Jeffares, A. Norman. 1968. *A Commentary on the Collected Poems of W. B. Yeats*. Stanford, California: Stanford University Press/

Marx, Karl, and Engels, Fredrich. 1848. "The Communist Manifesto," http://www.marxists.org/archive/marx/works/1848/communist-manifesto/. Accessed October 3, 2010. No pagination.

Miller, J. Hillis. 2001. "W. B. Yeats: 'The Cold Heaven.'" In *Others*. Princeton: Princeton University Press. 170-182.

Milton, John. 1674. *Paradise Lost*.

Nietzsche, Friedrich. *The Birth of Tragedy* and *The Case of Wagner*. Trans. Walter Kaufmann. New York: Vintage, 1967.

———. 1988a. *Die Geburt der Tragödie*. In *Sämtliche Werke*, Kritische Studienausgabe. Ed. Giorgio Colli and Mazzino Montinari. Munich, Berlin, New York: Walter de Gruyter. I: 9-156.

———. 1988b. "*Vom Nutzen und Nachtheil der Historie für das Leben*." In *Sämtliche Werke*, Kritische Studienausgabe. Ed. Giorgio Colli and Mazzino Montinari. Munich, Berlin, New York: Walter de Gruyter. I: 243-334.

———. 1988c. *Jenseits von Gut und Böse*. In *Sämtliche Werke*, Kritische Studienausgabe. Ed. Giorgio Colli and Mazzino Montinari. Munich, Berlin, New York: Walter de Gruyter. V: 9-243.

———. 1988d. "*Nachgelassene Fragmente 1869-1874*," In *Sämtliche Werke*, Kritische Studienausgabe. Ed. Giorgio Colli and Mazzino Montinari. Munich, Berlin, New York: Walter de Gruyter. VII.

———. 1995. "On the Utility and Liability of History for Life." Trans. Richard T. Gray. In *Unfashionable Observations*. In *The Complete Works*. Stanford, California: Stanford University Press. II: 83-167.

Shakespeare, William. 1597. *Romeo and Juliet*.

———. 1600. *As You Like It*.

———. 1606. *King Lear*.

Warminski, Andrzej. 1987. "Reading for Example: A Metaphor in Nietzsche's *Birth of Tragedy*." In *Readings in Interpretation: Hölderlin, Hegel, Heidegger*. Minneapolis: University of Minnesota Press. xxxv-lxi.

———. 1989. "Terrible Reading (preceded by 'Epigraphs')." In *Responses: Paul de Man's Wartime Journalism*. Lincoln: University of Nebraska Press. 386-96.

Yeats, W. B. 1977. *The Variorum Edition of the Poems*. Ed. Peter Allt and Russell K. Alspach. New York: Macmillan.

Permissions

Chapter One was first published in English as "Cold Heaven, Cold Comfort: Should We Read or Teach Literature Now?," in *The Edge of the Precipice: Why Read Literature in the Digital Age?*, ed. Paul Socken (Montreal & Kingston: McGill-Queen's University Press, 2013), 140-55. I am grateful to Paul Socken and the McGill-Queen's University Press for authorizing the translation into German of this essay and its publication in this volume.

Chapter Two was given in English in 2011 at the University of Konstanz as the First Annual Wolfgang Iser Memorial lecture and then translated into German by Monika Reif-Hülser as "Grenzgänge mit Iser und Coetzee: Literature lessen—aber Wie und Wozu?" trans. Monika Reif-Hülser. I thank Professor Reif-Hülser for permission to reuse this essay in this volume.

Chapter Three was first published in English as "A Defense of Literary Study in a Time of Globalization and the New Teletechnologies," in *Translating Global Cultures: Toward Interdisciplinary (Re)Constructions*, ed. Wang Ning (Beijing: Foreign Language Teaching and Research Press, 2008), 29-46. I thank Wang Ning and Foreign Language and Teaching Research Press for authorizing the translation of this essay into German and its publication in this volume.

Chapter Four was first published in English as "Ecotechnics: Ecotechnological Odradek," as chapter two of *Telemorphosis: Theory in the Era of Climate*, Volume 1, ed. Tom Cohen (Ann Arbor, Michigan: Open Humanities Press, 2012), 65-103.

Chapter Five was first published as "Part I: Theories of Community," the first chapter of my *The Conflagration of Community: Fiction Before and After Auschwitz* (Chicago: University of Chicago Press, 2011), 1-35. © 2011 by The University of Chicago. All rights reserved. I am grateful to Alan G. Thomas, Perry Cartwright, and The University of Chicago Press for giving permission for its translation into German and its publication in this volume.

Chapter Six was first published as "Globalization and World Literature," *Neohelicon*, Special number on "Comparative Literature: Toward a (Re)construction of World Literature," Guest-edited by Wang Ning, vol. 38, No. 2 (2011), 251-265. I am grateful to Wang Ning, to the editor of Neohelicon, Peter Haidu, and to Akademiai Kiado for agreeing to the translation and publication in this volume of this essay in German.